The Tiffany Chapel at the MORSE MUSEUM

WITH CONTRIBUTIONS BY
Alice Cooney Frelinghuysen
Wendy Kaplan
Joel M. Hoffman
Rustin Levenson
John Maseman
Laurence J. Ruggiero
Patricia Pongracz Spicka
Thomas Venturella

EDITED BY
Nancy Long

© 2002 by The Charles Hosmer Morse Foundation, Inc., Winter Park, Florida
Design: Jacques Auger Design Associates, Inc.

Photographs of the Tiffany Chapel and other works in the Morse Museum of
American Art are by Eric Dusenbery, Dan Forer, Raymond Martinot and Allan
Maxwell for the Morse Museum.

On the Front Cover: *Tiffany Chapel Baptismal Font*, ca. 1892, with mosaic detail
of a chapel column in the background.

ISBN 0–9721437–0–X
Library of Congress Card Catalogue
Number 2002108196

TABLE
of Contents

Today it is difficult to appreciate fully the prescience of Hugh and Jeannette McKean nearly half a century ago when they stood amid the rubble of Tiffany's burned and forgotten Long Island estate and decided to save all they could. Among the many treasures they rescued was the chapel interior Tiffany had made in 1893 for the World's Columbian Exposition and in 1916 found necessary to rescue from neglect and deterioration at the Cathedral Church of Saint John the Divine.

Some four decades after Tiffany installed the chapel in an outbuilding on his estate, the McKeans discovered it was once again a sorely neglected work of art. Acquiring most of the remains at Laurelton Hall in 1957 and the remains of the chapel in 1959, they later added to their Tiffany collection through purchase and donation ultimately to form a wondrous collection of Tiffany material including some of his most important production.

Today we are in the midst of a Tiffany revival and reevaluation. It is an exciting time for Tiffany scholars and enthusiasts and a splendid moment to be advancing the dream of the McKeans to extend understanding and appreciation of late-nineteenth-century American art by presenting Tiffany's chapel interior to the public after a very long absence.

This book is really an accompaniment to the installation of that chapel in the Museum's north galleries. Part guide and part art history, its various chapters and authors illuminate aspects of the chapel in different ways. It is our hope that everyone will find something of interest and something that will enhance the understanding and appreciation of the work of Louis Tiffany.

Though more of the collection the McKeans amassed remains to be studied, prepared, and exhibited, the installation of the Tiffany Chapel represents a crucial step in realizing their dream of making their Tiffany holdings accessible to the public.

LAURENCE J. RUGGIERO
Director

INTRODUCTION

Louis Comfort Tiffany (1848-1933) was born to a legacy of wealth and matured in an era of prosperity, the post-Civil War Gilded Age. Fortunately for his own generation and those that have followed, he used his inheritance and family position to fulfill his insatiable desire to create beautiful things. His work, prodigious in output and encompassing most mediums, spanned five decades and three art movements.

Today art historians may debate whether his work influenced or was influenced by the Aesthetic, Arts and Crafts or Art Nouveau Movement, but there can be no doubt that it placed him solidly in a time of high energy and creative change in the visual arts.

During extensive travels in his 20s Tiffany immersed himself in the light of Egypt, Morocco, Tunisia, and Algeria. The exotic qualities of these cultures were both source and inspiration for him throughout his life. Although his first experiments with glass were in New York glass houses as early as 1872, his artistic career began as a painter. But as a partner in the firm Louis C. Tiffany & Co., Associated Artists (1879-1883), he turned from painting to design and created interiors for clients ranging from Mark Twain in Hartford, Connecticut, to President Chester Arthur at the White House.

In 1885 he established the firm Tiffany Glass Company, after he had earlier (1881) registered a patent for opalescent window glass. Opalescent glass was the result of a radical new technique whereby several colors and characteristics were combined and manipulated to create an unprecedented range of hues and three-dimensional effects.

While experimentation in glass and other mediums allowed Tiffany to produce unique objects as varied as an exquisite cloisonné jewel box and a great plated stained-glass window, his lifelong pursuit of unity in design was realized in mosaic. In 1893 a complex but unified vision of beauty inspired his chapel for the World's Columbian Exposition and finally in 1902-1905 this vision culminated in the last house he designed in its entirety— his own. The Morse Museum is the greatest repository of Tiffany furniture, stained glass, mosaic, and architectural elements from his residential masterpiece, Laurelton Hall, in Oyster Bay, Long Island. It was there that he installed his internationally acclaimed chapel, and now with its reassembly at the Morse Museum it can be experienced much as it was at the Chicago exposition.

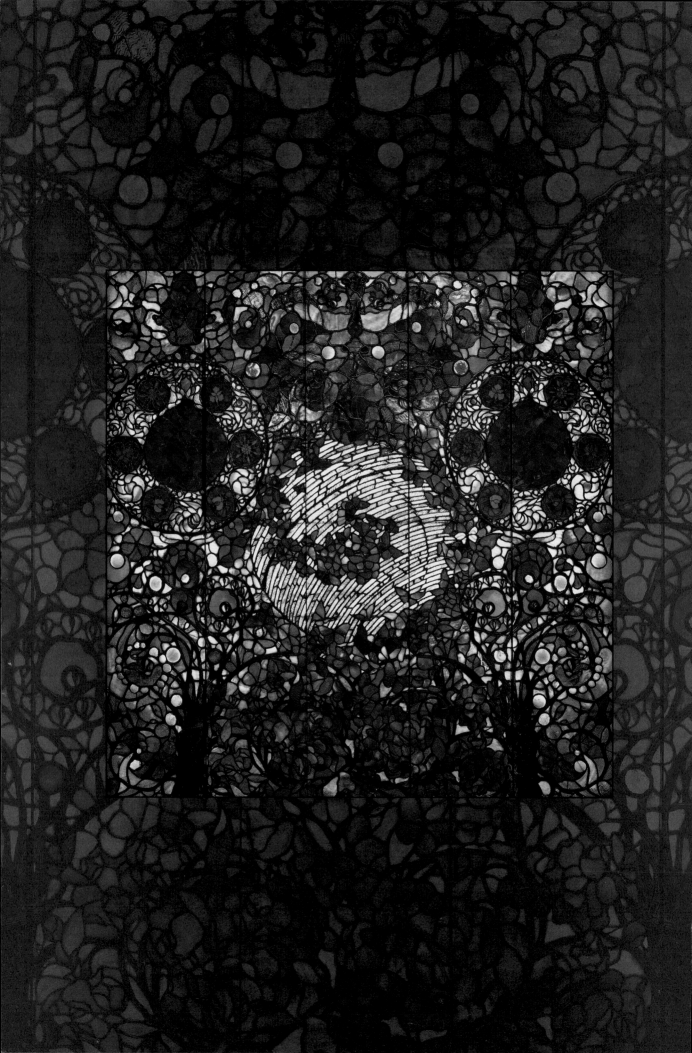

TIFFANY *and Design Reform*

by WENDY KAPLAN

Louis Comfort Tiffany's fifty-year career, which began in the 1870s, spanned the era of the nineteenth century's three most important design reform movements: Aesthetic, Arts and Crafts, and Art Nouveau. Until recently, most scholarship placed Tiffany firmly in the context of Art Nouveau.[1] The reasons for this association are clear. Practitioners of this "new art," which reached its height in the 1890s, were convinced that nature rather than historical styles should serve as the source of modern design. And Tiffany's aesthetic was based on this shared belief in nature as the primary font of design inspiration. Intoxicated by color, he translated into glass the lush palette found in flowers, plants, and wildlife. His glass was shown to great acclaim at the two most important exhibitions that served as international disseminators of Art Nouveau: the 1900 Paris Exposition Universelle and the 1902 Esposizione d'Arte Decorativa Moderna in Turin.

As historian Martin Eidelberg has argued, however, "Tiffany eschewed most of the bold ideas of High Art Nouveau, especially those of abstraction and linear dynamics....Tiffany in fact remained true to an older idea of beauty."[2] The call to nature, together with the desire to integrate art into everyday life, had been the principal catalyst for design reformers many years before the genesis of Art Nouveau. While Tiffany continued to work for two decades into the twentieth century, his taste and values were shaped most during the last decades of the nineteenth, when the Aesthetic Movement and then the Arts and Crafts were at their heights.

Placing Tiffany in the correct art historical category is not as important as understanding that his work held a significant place in the broader movement for design reform at the center of progressive artistic thinking from the 1860s to World War I. Although there are stylistic, chronological, and ideological differences among the various movements, these are more a question of emphasis rather than of kind. Articles by the leading advocates of Art Nouveau, such as the art dealer Siegfried Bing (whose Parisian gallery, L'Art Nouveau, gave the movement its name) and the French critic Jean Schopfer, demonstrate how closely the ideals of this movement echo those of the Arts and Crafts.

---

[1] The many books that consider Tiffany as an Art Nouveau designer include: Robert Koch, *Louis Comfort Tiffany: Rebel in Glass* (New York: Crown Publishers, 1982. Updated, third edition); Diane Chalmers Johnson, *American Art Nouveau* (New York: Abrams, 1979); and Robert Schmutzler, *Art Nouveau* (New York: Abrams, 1964).

[2] Martin Eidelberg, "Tiffany and the Cult of Nature" in Alastair Duncan et. al., *Masterworks of Louis Comfort Tiffany*, (New York: Harry N. Abrams, 1989), 88.

ing's article for *The Craftsman*, the most influential American journal of the Arts and Crafts Movement, attempts to define "what rules were to be observed" in following Art Nouveau principles.[3] His assertions confirm that the actual design philosophy of Art Nouveau continued the same proselytizing rhetoric that reformers had been expressing since the architect A.W.N. Pugin began championing the Gothic Revival in the 1830s. Bing states that designers should return to nature for inspiration and that objects be made with "honest" construction, fidelity to the inherent qualities of the material, and avoidance of unnecessary ornament. The Arts and Crafts Movement also adhered to these principles, and, with the exception of the prescription against ornament (or perhaps different criteria concerning what would make it "unnecessary"), so did the Aesthetic Movement. Bing became Tiffany's greatest champion in Europe: his gallery, which served as a conduit for the most innovative design at the turn of the century, was the only distributor of Tiffany's work on the Continent.[4] He wrote extensively about the glass in his publication of 1895, *La Culture artistique en Amérique*, and then in the first volume of the German periodical *Kunst und Kunsthandwerk*.[5] This influential article was translated into English in 1899, when it served as the introduction to an exhibition of Art Nouveau featuring Tiffany at the Grafton Galleries in London.

In 1903 Schopfer wrote a spirited defense of Art Nouveau in response to critics who had attacked it as a negative movement, united only by a shared rejection of historical styles. His statements concerning Art Nouveau principles are, again, indistinguishable from those describing the Arts and Crafts Movement. He draws the same conclusions as Bing, further emphasizing that Art Nouveau adherents considered the decorative arts to be of equal importance to the fine arts and encouraged the revival of activities in neglected areas such as textiles. He also claims that Art Nouveau is free of historical revivalism, although he conceded that it was influenced by many styles, particularly those from Japan.[6]

Unlike art historians today, critics at the turn of the century seemed more interested in defining principles rather than identifying specific design vocabularies. This explains why period accounts of world's fairs and expositions usually do not make stylistic distinctions between Walter Crane and Hector Guimard, or between William Morris and Victor Horta. They are all evaluated under the same rubric: as champions of "modern art."

The architect Guimard, who was himself a protagonist of French Art Nouveau, did the same. While acknowledging different manifestations of stylistic expression (he points out in an article of 1902, that in Belgium, "the decorative base is no longer the leaf and the flower, but simply the stem"), he places the efforts of English Arts and Crafts leaders such as Morris, Crane, and John Ruskin (who are now considered protagonists of the Aesthetic Movement as well), together with leaders of the Art Nouveau in France and Belgium. He evaluates all

[3] S. Bing, "L'Art Nouveau," *The Craftsman*, vol. 5 (October 1903), 1-15.

[4] In his gallery, Bing also showed the work of leading Arts and Crafts practitioners in Britain (such as William Morris and W.A.S. Benson) and the United States (such as the Grueby and Rookwood potteries).

[5] S. Bing, "Die Kunstglaser von Louis C. Tiffany," *Kunst und Kunsthandwerk* (Vol. 1, 1898), 105-111.

[6] Jean Schopfer, "L'Art Nouveau: An Argument in Defense," *The Craftsman*, vol. 4 (July 1903), 229-238. This article was written specifically in response to A.D.F. Hamlin, professor of art at Columbia University, who had written a scathing attack on the movement in the same journal: "L'Art Nouveau, Its Origins and Development," *The Craftsman*, vol. 3 (December 1902). 129-143.

their work as part of a quest to draw from nature in order to achieve a modern expression, a goal also held by Tiffany.[7] These shared objectives excited more comment than the differences between the Belgian proclivity to attenuate to complete abstraction the forms inspired by the stems of plants, the French tendency towards more naturalistic expressions, and the English distaste for anything too organic and flowing.

In sum, practitioners of the Aesthetic, Arts and Crafts, and Art Nouveau movements all believed in *Gesamtkunstwerk* (complete design unity), that the decorative arts were equal in importance to the fine arts, and that objects should be made "honestly" and be suitable for their intended purpose. A moral fervor about the "rightness" of this design philosophy permeated the movements. Furthermore, all three shared a conviction that the new industrial age must develop a modern art which would be freed from the shackles of the past. Stylistic liberation would be achieved by turning to first principles—whether to nature, to the vernacular, or to exotic and "primitive" cultures. Finally, the new art must be made more accessible; *how* it would be made was of great importance. This essay will examine where Tiffany fits into each of these vital issues of design reform.

While the overlaps in design philosophy among the reform movements are most significant, important distinctions must also be recognized. For example, Arts and Crafts leaders were more concerned with changing the nature of work, restoring the handmade in an increasingly industrialized society, and using furnishings as a means of social uplift. Art Nouveau proponents cared most about rejecting historical styles, embracing nature as the primary design source, and establishing a modern art that would define the age. In the Aesthetic Movement, the decorated surface was the very essence of an object's appearance, in contrast to Art Nouveau's and Arts and Crafts' promotion of simplicity as an ideal. Which aspects of the three movements are characteristic of Tiffany's own convictions and practices?

As suggested earlier, Tiffany was most committed to the central issues of the Aesthetic Movement. His life was devoted to "The Quest for Beauty"—the title of an elaborate pageant he staged in 1916 and of an article he wrote for *Harper's Bazaar* in 1917. These ideals were first formulated some eighty years earlier. In 1835 the French poet and critic Theophile Gautier declared that art cannot nor should be in any way useful; there must only be "Art for Art's Sake" (*"L'Art pour L'Art"*). Aestheticism was codified in 1873, when the Oxford don Walter Pater declared the supremacy of "the desire of beauty, the love of art for art's sake." [8]

The belief that the artist's only duty was to beauty and to his own self expression was always an extreme ideal. Matthew Arnold, the English poet, essayist, and educator, best articulated the defining qualities of the Aesthetic Movement. He advocated what he termed "sweetness and light." Sweetness was the desire to enhance life though art, but this impulse to create beauty had to be accompanied by light, which he expressed as the desire "to see and learn the truth and make it prevail."[9] Therefore education, social reform, and a rejection of dogmatism must be

[7] Hector Guimard, "An Architect's Opinion of L'Art Nouveau," *The Architectural Record*, vol.12 (June 1902), 127. The designer Alexandre Charpentier expresses similar opinions in another article about Art Nouveau in the same issue of this journal, placing a greater emphasis on the necessity for an art that can be shared by all. He quotes from William Morris, and then asserts: "The art of the future must be a democratic art." 122-125.

[8] Quoted in Lionel Lambourne, *The Aesthetic Movement* (London: Phaidon Press, 1996), 10, 12.

[9] Quoted in Mark Girouard, *Sweetness and Light: The Queen Anne Movement, 1860–1900* (Oxford University Press, 1977), 4. Arnold coined the phrase "sweetness and light" in his influential book *Culture and Anarchy* (1869).

1. Louis Comfort Tiffany's studio at the Charles Lewis Tiffany 72nd Street mansion, New York City, designed 1883. From the article "The Most Artistic House in New York" printed in *Ladies' Home Journal*, vol. 17, no. 12, Nov. 1900, page 13. Morse Museum of American Art.

part of the enlightenment that would beautify one's existence. (Only the most notorious aesthetes were advocates of sweetness alone.) Tiffany best fits the model of sweetness with light: beauty and nature were his twin gods, and he remained a faithful acolyte throughout his life. His vast inherited wealth gave him the freedom to remain uncompromising in his exacting standards for quality.

Tiffany's interiors, especially for his own residences, are triumphs of design unity (fig. 1). The ideal of *Gesamtkunstwerk* was the creation of a total work of art, where the building, its furnishings, and its landscape form an environmental whole. This impulse emerged as a reaction against the cacophony of classical revival styles, ranging from Louis XIV to the Rococo Revival, that dominated

the architecture and decorative arts of the nineteenth century. Throughout his career, however, instead of following the Art Nouveau rejection of past styles, Tiffany retained the discriminating eclecticism that characterized the Aesthetic Movement. As historian Alice Cooney Frelinghuysen has pointed out, "he drew on exotic and historical sources and was attracted to the arts of China, Japan, ancient Greece, Egypt, Venice, India, and the world of Islam."[10]

Tiffany developed a commitment to unified artistic expression early in his career. Like so many reformers, he followed the model of the artist-turned-designer, with the conviction that furnishings were not only as aesthetically valid as paintings or sculpture, but also that these objects provided a more complete artistic experience. Originally trained as a painter, he began studying the chemistry and techniques of glass-making when he was twenty-four. Sympathetic to

[10] Alice Cooney Frelinghuysen, "Louis Comfort Tiffany at The Metropolitan Museum of Art," *The Metropolitan Museum of Art Bulletin,* vol. 56 (Summer 1998), 4.

2. Tiffany-designed drawing room in Mark Twain House, Hartford, Connecticut, 1874. Mark Twain House.

3. Veteran's Room, Seventh Regiment Armory, New York City. Designed by Louis C. Tiffany and Associated Artists, 1879-80. Archival photograph, The New-York Historical Society.

British ideals about art industry, Tiffany became a member of textile designer Candace Wheeler's New York Society of Decorative Arts in 1878 (Wheeler had been deeply influenced by Morris and Crane). The following year he informed her: "I have been thinking a great deal about decorative work, and I am going into it as a profession. I believe there is more in it than in painting pictures."[11] Wheeler, Lockwood de Forest, and Samuel Colman joined Tiffany in this venture, which provided him with the first opportunity to apply his experiments with glass. Between 1879 and 1883, they designed innovative interior decoration for clients ranging from Mark Twain in Hartford, Connecticut (fig. 2), to the Seventh Regiment Armory in New York (fig. 3) and even President Chester Arthur at the White House.

In 1885 Tiffany established the Tiffany Glass Company, and while he continued to undertake decorating commissions, his focus was on new methods of glass manufacture. Four years earlier he had registered a patent for opalescent window glass, a radical new treatment whereby several colors were combined and manipulated to create an unprecedented range of hues and three-dimensional effects. Tiffany believed that this new material allowed more fidelity to the inherent nature of the medium, because it enabled form to be defined by the glass itself rather than by painting *onto* the glass (fig. 4).

Opalescent glass, however, was firmly rejected by the other important school of the stained-glass revival, which advocated the Gothic tradition of painting with enamel on clear, uniformly colored "antique" glass. The passionate moral dimension of late-nineteenth-century taste is clearly seen in Boston glassmaker Charles Connick's declaration that his firm's greatest contribution to stained glass was "rescuing it from the abysmal depth of opalescent picture windows."[12] Those, like Connick, who followed the medieval precedent of painting on clear glass, were in bitter opposition to Tiffany and to John La Farge, the artist who had developed opalescent glass about the same time as Tiffany, and was his chief competitor.

Both schools thought that they alone were being "truthful," an ideal central to the philosophy of the Aesthetic and Arts and Crafts movements. Connick was a protégé of architect Ralph Adams Cram, the leading American advocate of the Gothic Revival and a founding member of the Society of Arts and Crafts in Boston. Cram's opposition to Tiffany windows demonstrates how divergent in beliefs design reform movements could be. Cram maintained that stained glass was not supposed to function as a picture, since truth to materials would

[11] Candace Wheeler, *Yesterday in a Busy Life* (New York and London: Harper & Brothers, 1918), 231.

[12] "Famed Stained Glass Expert is Dead at 70," obituary for Charles Connick, *Boston Herald*, December 29, 1945.

4. Louis Comfort Tiffany. Tiffany Studios. *Butterfly* window for Tiffany mansion, 72nd Street, New York City, ca. 1885. Leaded Favrile glass, 65 x 63 in. (165.1 x 161.3 cm). Morse Museum of American Art (60-006).

dictate that it serve only as a translucent wall. Furthermore, he rejected Tiffany's glass because it "was based on entirely new principles wholly at variance both with those held during the great five hundred years of the middle ages and with the whole ethos of Christian art."[13]

In contrast, Tiffany was intensely proud of the pictorial quality of his glass, of the eclectic nature of his design sources (as opposed to a strict adherence to the Gothic, especially for churches), and above all, of his novel materials and techniques. Embracing the principles of the new art, he declared himself to be "untrammeled by tradition and moved solely by a desire to produce a thing of beauty." And unlike Gothic Revival purists, he was not opposed to new materials, proclaiming that his innovations were made possible by "the aid of modern chemistry."[14]

Cram scored at least one major victory over

Tiffany. As Patricia Spicka describes in greater detail in the chapter "The Chapel's First Installation and Move to Saint John the Divine" in this book, Chicago philanthropist Celia Whipple Wallace had purchased the famous chapel Tiffany constructed for his display at the 1893 World's Columbian Exposition in Chicago for installation in the Cathedral Church of Saint John the Divine in New York City. There its dazzling mosaics shone in all their Byzantine-style splendor. But when Cram's firm became the cathedral architects in 1911 and the nave was built, Cram made sure that Tiffany's chapel was sealed off and rendered unusable.[15]

Tiffany's passion for unity, first manifested in his efforts to create complete interiors, was subsequently extended to the design and manufacture of his stained glass. The leading necessary to hold the pieces of glass together became a fully integrated design element, simulating, for example, the stems of plants. A window that Tiffany designed for the Paris world's fair of 1900 exemplifies his aesthetic (fig. 5). It depicts the subject Tiffany loved most—nature, in this case, the transformation wrought by the changing seasons. No paint at all was applied to *The Four Seasons*: the delineation of clouds, branches, flowers, fruits, and vegetables was achieved through the leading. Tiffany did his best work when free from the restrictions of his ecclesiastical commissions, which often demanded traditional religious figural scenes. He vastly preferred landscapes, where he could present the

13 Quoted in Koch 1982, 80.

14 Louis Comfort Tiffany, "American Art Supreme in Colored Glass" *The Forum* (July 1893), 623.

15 In 1916 Tiffany removed the chapel from the cathedral and installed it on the grounds of Laurelton Hall, his estate on Long Island. In 1958 the collector and Tiffany biographer Hugh McKean purchased the by-then severely damaged chapel and gave it to the museum he directed in Winter Park, Florida. Now fully restored in the Morse Museum of American Art, the chapel is again open to the public.

5. Louis C. Tiffany. Tiffany Glass and Decorating Company. *The Four Seasons* window as shown in the Exposition Universelle, Paris, 1900. Leaded Favrile glass, approximately 107 x 92 in. (271.8 x 233.7 cm). From *The Art Work of Louis C. Tiffany* by Charles de Kay, 1914, copy #1. Morse Museum of American Art (69-017).

glorious bounty of nature solely with pieces of plated and manipulated pot-metal glass.

The window was displayed at the entrance to the American section of the fair, and was hailed by critics as the best art the country had to offer. It was then shown at two other world's fairs: the 1901 Pan-American in Buffalo and at Turin in 1902. *The Four Seasons* had such resonance for Tiffany that he subsequently divided the window into individual panels and installed them in the living room at Laurelton Hall, his home in Oyster Bay, Long Island (fig. 6).

The house was the culmination of his desire to create unified artistic statements. Completed in 1905, it was the last house he designed in its entirety.

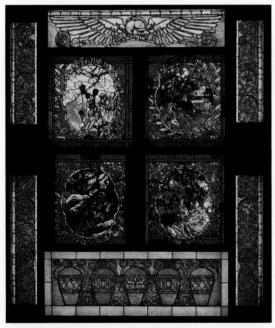

6. Louis C. Tiffany. Tiffany Glass and Decorating Company. Panels from *The Four Seasons* window, ca. 1892, as displayed at the Morse Museum of American Art. Leaded Favrile glass. *Spring*, 39 1/8 x 37 3/4 in. (99.5 x 95.9 cm) (57-018); *Summer*, 39 1/8 x 37 3/4 in. (99.4 x 95.9 cm) (57-017); *Autumn*, 39 7/8 x 36 3/8 in. (101.3 x 92.4 cm) (57-019); *Winter*, 39 5/8 x 33 in. (100.6 x 83.8 cm) (62-033); *Eagle* (57-020) 17 x 80 in. (43.2 x 203.2 cm); Borders (64-036 A&B) 45 x 13 2/5 in. (114.3 x 34 cm); Borders (64-036 C&D) 57 x 13 2/5 in. (144.8 x 34 cm); Urns (U-083) 28 x 84 in. (71.1 x 213.4 cm). Morse Museum of American Art.

A deeply cherished belief in design reform circles was that the worth of an object should be measured by the creativity and skill in its execution rather than the monetary value of its materials. Tiffany was in total accord with this principle, as demonstrated in his use of "found" materials: pebbles in stained glass windows (fig. 7), stones on ornamented doors for the 1892 Havemeyer house, the use of wine caskets as interior decoration in his own apartment, and the preference for semi-precious stones such as opals in his jewelry (fig. 8). Like Arts and Crafts aficionados, he valued materials native to a particular region, and chose to depict native wildflowers over cultivated ones.

Tiffany came closest to the ideals of the Arts and Crafts Movement when he extended his commitment to unity in design to include unity in how things were made. Tiffany was convinced that the production of a stained-glass window required the artist's involvement at every stage, even in a factory setting—from creating the first sketches to overseeing how the glass was selected, cut, and assembled.

The greatest fear of Arts and Crafts proponents was that the industrial process had stripped the craftsperson of his or her individuality; they vowed to change society by changing the nature of work. They believed that if objects were again made by hand, "joy in labor" would be restored, and shoddy work would disappear. By all accounts Tiffany's workplaces came closer than most to fulfilling William Morris' dream of "A Factory as It Might Be."[16]

In the face of increasing mechanization and division of labor in the glass industry, Tiffany workers were trained to be "all-round men, working in harmony," as the English critic Cecilia Waern observed in 1897. She attests to the supremacy of hand work in the making of glass, even in the context of large-scale production. While Tiffany maintained overall creative control, his workplace "allow[ed] for personal interest on the part of the worker" in the production of windows as well as "Favrile" glass (fig. 9).[17] In 1893 Tiffany had introduced his first blown-glass vases and bowls whose name, Favrile, he declared, was taken from an old English word for handmade. Favrile glass quickly gained international renown for its surface iridescence and brilliant colors (fig. 10).

In an article the following year Waern discusses the participation of female craftspeople manipulating the pieces of glass mosaic: "The young women working under Mr. Tiffany's directions use them with admirable patience, dexterity, and freedom. It is a real work of translation...."[18] Although no worker was permitted to affix his or her name to an object, considerable freedom must have been the *modus operandi*, since, for example, the firm maintained as a point of pride that no two pieces of Favrile were alike and at its peak, the factory at Corona, New York, produced over thirty thousand pieces of glass a year.

Despite this close adherence to Arts and Crafts principles of hand work and pride in the process of making, Tiffany was not really considered part of the movement. Referring to Tiffany as a key exemplar of

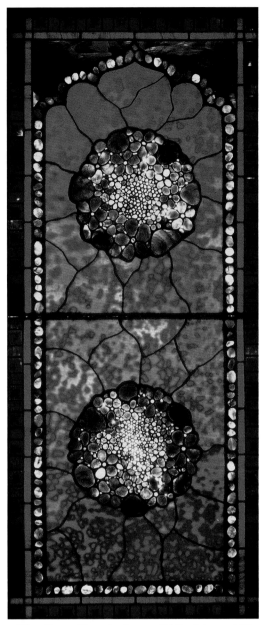

7. Tiffany Glass and Decorating Company, *Pebble* window, ca. 1885 or 1890s. Clear and colored glass and pebbles, 59 5/8 x 25 3/8 in. (151.4 x 65.4 cm). Morse Museum of American Art (58-016).

[16] This ideal was expressed in an essay of 1884: "A Factory as It Might Be," in May Morris, ed., *William Morris: Artist, Writer, Socialist* (reprint, New York: Russel and Russel, 1966), 130-40.

[17] Cecilia Waern, "The Industrial Arts of America: the Tiffany Glass and Decorative Co.," *The Studio*, vol. 11 (September 1897), 157.

[18] Cecilia Waern, "The Industrial Arts of America: II. The Tiffany or 'Favrile' Glass," *The Studio*, vol. 14 (June 1898), 18.

American industrial arts, Waern asks: "And why not say the Arts and Crafts?" She answers by insisting that America lacked "the social gospel that lies at the heart of the English movement, the noble desire for the regeneration of society on widespread and practical lines...." Including Louis' father (the impresario of the famous silver and jewelry emporium) in the discussion, she explicates further: "The Tiffanys certainly do not try to emulate Morris and Company in educating the public taste; their aim is to sell, to persuade, not to elevate or instruct." [19]

While it is undoubtedly true that Tiffany did not share the passion for a more equitable distribution of goods that led Morris to join the Socialist party in 1883, he did embrace the moral aesthetics of the Arts and Crafts Movement. This was the ideal that living with beautiful objects, or filling public spaces with them, would make people not only feel better but *be* better as well—that, somehow, beauty was inherently improving. In 1885, *The New York Times* saw Tiffany's interior for the Lyceum Theater in New York as "something more than a carnal pleasure of the eye or a sensuous luxury; it rises to the level of instruction." [20]

In contrast to Waern, other critics compared

8. Louis Comfort Tiffany, designer; Julia Sherman (worked ca. 1902-1914), maker, Tiffany & Co. *The Peacock Necklace*, ca. 1906. Obverse: opals, cloisonné enamel, sapphires, amethysts, demantoid garnets, yellow sapphires, rubies, emerald, and pearls. Reverse: cloisonné enamel on gold, H: 7 in. x L: 10 in. (19.1 x 25.4 cm). Morse Museum of American Art (58-001).

Tiffany favorably to Morris. In the June 1899 issue of *Brush and Pencil*, after extolling Morris' genius for combining the fine with the "useful" arts, Gardner Teall asserted that "Louis C. Tiffany has probably done the most of any one practically toward forwarding a feeling for the beautiful as applied to our necessities....He has not been content with the mere discovery of things, but like Morris he has spent quite as much energy in applying his art and doing that unselfishly...." [21] In the *Fine Arts Journal* for April 1908, University of Chicago professor Edmund Buckley wrote a lengthy article about the Tiffany mosaic ceiling for Chicago's Marshall Field department store. He enthuses, "one may see in this mart of trade where people most do congregate, one step forward in realization of William Morris' prediction, 'Some day we shall win back art, that is to say, the pleasure of life, to the people.'" Fully acknowledging the ceiling's great expense (a quarter of a million dollars, which in today's terms would be many times that figure), Buckley insists that the money was well spent because, "under the current competitive and individualistic social system, the poor will always be with us and that no

9. Above: The Glass Shop, Tiffany Studios, 1913. From *Character and Individuality in Decorations and Furnishings* catalogue, Tiffany Studios. Morse Museum of American Art.

10. Right: Louis Comfort Tiffany. Tiffany Studios. *Jack-in-the-Pulpit* vase, ca. 1913. Favrile glass, 18 x 10 in. (47 x 25.4 cm). Morse Museum of American Art (54-026).

[19] Waern 1897, 156 and 162.

[20] Quoted in Neil Harris, "Louis Comfort Tiffany: The Search for Influence" in Duncan et.al. 1989, 34.

11. Tiffany Studios, Abalone Desk Set, ca. 1920. Gilt bronze and abalone (left to right, top to bottom) Calendar (Perpetual), 5 3/4 x 6 1/2 in. (14.6 x 16.5 cm) (68-003:10); Utility Box, 1 1/4 x 5 1/2 x 3 1/2 in. (3.2 x 14 x 8.9 cm) (68-003:14); Paperweight, 1 7/8 x 3 3/4 x 3 3/4 in. (4.8 x 9.5 x 9.5 cm) (77-015); Paper Knife, 10 in. (25.4 cm) (68-003:07); Memoranda Pad, 7 1/2 x 4 3/4 x 1/8 in. (19.1 x 12.1 x 0.3 cm) (68-003:12). Morse Museum of American Art.

quarter million, no nor quarter billion, could give them more than very temporary betterment; and that this uplift will itself promote the reform needed to render the poor for evermore impossible."[22] Even Matthew Arnold could have offered no greater justification that "light" was itself intrinsic to "sweetness."

Following this line of reasoning, Tiffany's mass-produced objects for the home joined his windows and mosaics designed for public spaces as exemplars of the ameliorating power of art. Desktop items in metal were introduced about 1897, after a foundry was added to the glass furnaces in Corona (fig. 11); leaded lamps were offered commercially about a year later. The lamps, desk sets, and other metal objects such as candelabra

were not custom pieces; they were made in the thousands. The metal was cast or spun, not worked by hand. Even the leaded-glass shades were repetitions of a standard pattern (fig. 12). All formed part of what historian Neil Harris has called "personalized industrial production, an aggressively marketed workshop output achieved by designer and worker collaboration."[23]

In 1914 Tiffany commissioned a limited-edition biography from critic Charles de Kay. *The Art Work of Louis C. Tiffany* demonstrated his adherence to the *sine qua non* of design reformers, "that things of daily use like lamps, flower-vases, and toilet articles reach a wider public than

[21] Gardner C. Teall, "The Art of Things," *Brush and Pencil*, vol. 4 (Sept. 1899), 310-311.

[22] Edmund Buckley, "Artistic Aspects of America's Greatest Store, *"Fine Arts Journal* (April 1908), 206.

do paintings and sculpture make the 'decorative' arts more important to a nation than the 'fine arts.'" Not only were decorative artists "educators of the people in the truest sense," but the objects themselves, even when one-of-a-kind, served a proselytizing function. De Kay declares that each piece of Tiffany's jewelry (a medium he first displayed in 1904), "acts as a little missionary of art and tries in its own dumb way to convert the Philistine."[24]

Influenced by de Kay's authorized assessment and by his own idealized image of Tiffany, Hugh McKean's biography also presents this image of consumer democracy. Tiffany's own daughter, however, disagreed. After reading McKean's book in 1976, she wrote to him, " you have been able to picture him consistently as anxious to better the world.... All along I have had difficulty in seeing my father as inspired by [this] wish....I have seen him much more as giving in to an insatiable urge to express the ideas which flooded his mind."[25]

Although his status as a representative of democratic design has been debated, both contemporary scholarship and period accounts are in agreement that Tiffany's overarching goal was to express himself as an artist, and that his unique

12. Louis Comfort Tiffany. Tiffany Studios. *Dragonfly lamp*, after 1902. Leaded Favrile glass and doré bronze base, 27 x 20 diameter in. (68.6 x 50.8 diameter cm). Morse Museum of American Art (69-003).

contribution was his dazzling effects with colored glass. His passionate perfectionism was legendary. Glassblower Jimmy Stewart recalled: "Couldn't find no seconds in Tiffany....Every piece that went out was first-class, and if it wasn't they'd break it up." An anecdote told by another former employee is especially telling: "Mr. Tiffany was a nice man but a hard man to work for. One day we were running tests on a batch of glaze, Mr. Tiffany was there—he was always there—when a worker dropped a cigar stub out of his pocket into the vat. I figured to pick it out but Mr. Tiffany raged at the worker and ordered the entire batch destroyed."[26]

Tiffany himself seemed ambivalent about his not-always-complementary roles of artist and entrepreneur. His stained-glass windows and mosaics were always custom-made, very expensive, and unless designed for a church or a public building (such as the Marshall Field department store), could be enjoyed only by the privileged few. While he used sophisticated marketing techniques for more mass-produced items—widely distributing company catalogues, "planting" laudatory articles in magazines, and maintaining elaborate showrooms—his

[23] Harris in Duncan, et.al. 1989, 37.

[24] [Charles de Kay], *The Art Work of Louis C. Tiffany* (Garden City, New York: Doubleday, Page & Company, 1914), 27-28 and 35.

[25] Unpublished letter from Dorothy Burlingham to Hugh McKean, August 25, 1976. Archives, The Morse Museum of American Art.

intended clientele was still elite. An 1896 advertisement said that Tiffany's Favrile glass was
"most appropriate for collectors and lovers of
art,"[27] further suggesting its limited market. The
same, however, would apply to William Morris'
various endeavors. Even Morris textiles and wall-
papers would not have been accessible to most
people.

Tiffany's work reflects the efforts to
resolve the conflicting ideals of design reform
movements. William Morris had declared: "I do
not want art for a few, any more than education
for a few, or freedom for a few."[28] Yet most com-
panies could not produce affordable art for the
home while retaining high standards and individual
expression. Tiffany triumphed where others had
failed because his personal fortune allowed him
to sacrifice company profits in the interest of
artistic achievement. In addition, he provided an
extraordinary range of products, so that at least
middle-class consumers, if not the masses, had
access to his religion of beauty.

Tiffany is best understood in the context
of a broad definition of design reform. His work
bridges aspects of the Aesthetic, Arts and Crafts,
and Art Nouveau movements. Having spent a
lifetime insisting on the uniqueness of his artistic
vision and his very individualistic passion for
color, light, and nature, Tiffany would not allow
himself to be fit into any neat category. But perhaps
more than any other American designer at the

turn of the century, he succeeded in the ideal of
marrying art and industry. His long career bears
testament to the realization of the goal he first
outlined in the late 1870s: "We are going after
the money there is in art, but the art is there, all
the same."[29]

[26] Robert Koch, *Louis C. Tiffany's Glass, Bronzes, Lamps* (New York: Crown Publishers, 1971), 72 and 150.

[27] Advertisement, Tiffany Glass and Decorating Company. From *Art Interchange* 36 (February 1896), vi.

[28] This is from an 1877 lecture, "The Lesser Arts," reprinted in G.D.H. Cole, ed., *William Morris: Selected Writings*. (London: Nonesuch Press, 1948), 514.

[29] Candace Wheeler recalls this conversation with Tiffany in Wheeler 1918, 232.

A Tiffany Masterpiece REDISCOVERED

by LAURENCE J. RUGGIERO

As with the reputations of many artists now regarded as great masters, the reputation of Louis Comfort Tiffany waxed, waned, and then reemerged to dazzle again. When this happens to a painter or a sculptor, there are bound to be losses. But since people tend to banish unwanted paintings or sculptures to some attic or cellar, there is hope. For the maker of interiors, unhappy fate often means not banishment but annihilation. Unfortunately for Tiffany, interiors were among his most impressive achievements.

The best-known and most-accessible surviving residential interior by Tiffany is probably the Mark Twain House in Hartford, Connecticut (see fig. 2). This was done in 1881 before Tiffany's artistic maturity, during the time he was active in the Associated Artists from 1881 to 1883. Gone, however, are his own houses, the H. O. Havemeyer House and many other Tiffany interiors.

The 1993 exhibition "Splendid Legacy: The Havemeyer Collection" at the Metropolitan Museum of Art focused attention on the lost interior made for the Havemeyer house—lost to the wrecking ball in 1930[1]. This increased understanding of Louis Tiffany as a designer of interiors.

Tiffany's reputation, however, was restored and has grown in recent years largely on the basis of individual objects that have survived. Splendid leaded-glass windows—notably the View of Oyster Bay *(fig. 13) window at The Metropolitan Museum of Art[2] and the* Wisteria *(fig. 14) windows from the dining room at Tiffany's last, most-elaborate home[3]—have found a grandly generous reception, as have lamps. Today they have assumed a place of great affection in the hearts and minds of a large public—a public which has reflected its opinion in rising prices and an apparently boundless demand for exhibitions and reproductions of Tiffany's work.*

[1] Alice Cooney Frelinghuysen, Gary Tinterow, Susan Alyson Stein, Gretchen Wold, Julia Meech, *Splendid Legacy: The Havemeyer Collection*. This publication was issued in conjunction with the exhibition "Splendid Legacy: The Havemeyer Collection" held at The Metropolitan Museum of Art, New York, from March 27 to June 20, 1993.

[2] The *View of Oyster Bay* leaded-glass window, Louis Comfort Tiffany, 1905, on permanent loan to The Metropolitan Museum of Art from The Charles Hosmer Morse Museum of American Art.

[3] Seven of the eight *Wisteria* leaded-glass transoms Louis Comfort Tiffany made for his dining room at Laurelton Hall, 1903, are in the collection of the Morse Museum. The eighth is in the Anchorman Collection, Nagoya, Japan.

With public interest and scholarly investigation into the American Arts and Crafts and American Aesthetic movements[4], Tiffany has reemerged as a major American designer even without truly comprehensive knowledge or even broad awareness of his greatest achievements as a maker of whole interiors.

This situation makes the reassembly of the original main elements of one of Tiffany's greatest interiors—his chapel of 1893—not only exciting but important.

Although still more about Tiffany's chapel remains to be learned, the basic outlines of the chapel's history are pretty clear.

Louis Comfort Tiffany installed his chapel in the Manufactures and Liberal Arts Building at the world's fair, called the World's Columbian

13. Louis Comfort Tiffany. Tiffany Studios. *View of Oyster Bay* window, ca. 1908. From the William C. Skinner House, New York City. Leaded Favrile glass, 72 3/4 x 66 1/2 in. (184.8 x 168.9 cm). Lent to The Metropolitan Museum of Art by the Morse Museum of American Art in memory of Charles Hosmer Morse. (69-001); (MET Loan # L.1978.19).

Exposition, held from May to October in Chicago in 1893. A late entrant to the fair, Tiffany used space reserved by his father for Tiffany & Co. and installed the work of his own company, Tiffany Glass and Decorating Company.

In Chicago, the fairgrounds extended over six hundred and thirty acres and included more than two hundred buildings. Inside the buildings were machines, art objects, furnishings, and exhibits of every variety ranging from the ridiculous to the sublime—all much to the delight of the fair's twenty-seven million visitors.

The 1893 fair was the site of the debut of exotic dancer Little Egypt, George W. Ferris' great iron Ferris Wheel designed to outshine Eiffel's tower for the 1889 fair—though it never did—and Colgate toothpaste. With the exception of the great golden doors Louis Sullivan designed for the Transportation Building, the Columbian Exposition is remembered by most as a grand old-fashioned fair with no end of novelties. Architecturally, however, the fair looked backward rather than forward.

This is a surprising context for a true masterpiece of American design which brought European as well as American prominence to its creator.

But this was exactly what happened when the Tiffany Glass and Decorating Company, later renamed Tiffany Studios, created a major exhibit for the occasion. The heart of Louis Comfort Tiffany's exhibit was a chapel filled with ecclesiastical furnishings, costumes, and liturgical objects as well as leaded-glass windows,

[4] For a brief introduction of the Arts and Crafts movement, see Elizabeth Cumming and Wendy Kaplan, *The Arts and Crafts Movement* (London and New York: Thames and Hudson, 1991). In connection with the American Aesthetic movement see Doreen Bolger Burke, Jonathan Freedman, Alice Cooney Frelinghuysen, David A. Hanks, Marilyn Johnson, James D. Kornwolf, Catherine Lynn, Roger B. Stein, Jennifer Toher, and Catherine Hoover Voorsanger, with the assistance of Carrie Rebora, *In Pursuit of Beauty: Americans and the Aesthetic Movement* published in conjunction with the exhibition "In Pursuit of Beauty: Americans and the Aesthetic Movement" held at The Metropolitan Museum of Art, New York, from October 23, 1986 to January 11, 1987.

precious mosaics, and an elaborate altar. It was approximately thirty-seven feet long, twenty-four feet wide and rose at its highest point to twenty-four feet. It included a baptistery to the side and was agreed at the time to be sublime. It appealed across all categories of fairgoers—American and foreign, the wealthy and those of modest means, people who knew and loved Tiffany's work, and people who had never before seen it. The exhibit established Tiffany internationally and set the stage for more than a decade of astonishing commercial as well as artistic success.

Tiffany knew that to participate in the Chicago world's fair was to take a deliberate step into the inter-

national arena as well as to expand and deepen his presence in America. After all, world's fairs were a major vehicle for spreading technology, trade, and ideas across borders in the early days of globalization.

After the fair, Tiffany glass became readily available all over America. It was sold at fine department stores and exclusive shops as well as at Tiffany & Co. and Tiffany Studios in New York. In Europe it was sold by Siegfried Bing, the famous founder of the Paris shop L'Art Nouveau, which gave that movement its name.

At the peak of Tiffany's popularity from the mid-1890s through most of the first decade of the twentieth century, ownership of Tiffany glass was the aspiration of every middle-class American and an essential for museums and collectors throughout Europe. Tiffany glass was also at that time the inspira-

14. Louis Comfort Tiffany. Tiffany Studios. *Wisteria* windows, ca. 1910, as displayed at the Morse Museum of American Art. From the dining room of Laurelton Hall, Long Island, New York. Leaded Favrile glass (left to right, top to bottom), 38 x 71 1/2 in. (96.5 x 181.6 cm) (58-014); 36 7/8 x 96 5/8 in. (93.6 x 245.4 cm) (59-010); 36 3/4 x 69 3/4 x 1 1/2 in. (93.3 x 177.2 x 3.8 cm) (59-011); 36 5/8 x 44 3/4 x 1 1/4 in. (93 x 113.7 x 3.2 cm) (59-009:B); 36 x 48 x 1 3/4 in. (91.4 x 121.9 x 4.4 cm) (59-009:A); 36 x 47 x 1 in. (92.7 x 120.7 x 2.5 cm) (59-009:C). Morse Museum of American Art.

tion of designers from California to Czechoslovakia.

For a variety of reasons little visual documentary material of the chapel has survived. The key images are a chromolithograph of an 1893 watercolor (fig. 15) by an artist associated with the Tiffany Glass and Decorating Company, and two photographs of the interior of the Manufactures Building in the collections of the Chicago Historical Society (fig. 16) and the Morse Museum of American Art (fig. 17). Accounts at the time, though almost unanimous in their praise, are often inaccurate or contradictory in detail. The Museum's installation of the chapel elements relies to a large extent on the surviving architectural elements themselves and Tiffany's own later restoration and reinstallation of the chapel on the grounds of his estate in Oyster Bay, Long Island, as well as what documentary information survives from 1893.

In trying to project what it must have been like to enter the chapel in 1893 Robert Koch, one of the earliest Tiffany scholars, said, "[it] may very well have been an experience similar to that encountered by the people of Ravenna [Italy] when their own

16. Tiffany Glass and Decorating Company's Tiffany Chapel installation in the Manufactures and Liberal Arts Building, from upper level showing mural on facade and small building housing the baptistery attached to the south face, 1893. Chicago Historical Society.

15. After Joseph Lauber (1855-1948). *Tiffany Chapel*, ca. 1893. Chromolithograph, 10 x 8 in. (25.4 x 20.3 cm). Morse Museum of American Art (68-007).

mosaics were new." "The chapel," he continued, "was opulent without ostentation, the static structural forms made vibrant with luminous color."[5]

The chapel is really an ensemble of magnificently decorated and integrated architectural elements set in an intimate simple space. It is a tour de force of mosaic, a virtuoso performance in glass, and a sculptural achievement in a brilliantly unified design. Its underlying geometry of rectangles, cylinders, spheres, and squares is as simple as its decoration is complex. Tiffany exercised complete control over these elements. The resulting unity of his design is ultimately the quality that makes this chapel one of his greatest creations, one of the finest monuments of the period, and one that is awe-inspiring still.

Tiffany built his chapel up from simple columns and arches that were massive in size relative to the small, intimate dimensions of the space in which he put them. This produced dramatic light and shadow effects that stunned visitors who suddenly found themselves in a distinctly different world—a world that enveloped them and though very small (approximately one thousand square feet), seemed to dwarf them.

On the basic structural elements of the columns and arches, and then on the furniture, fixtures, and walls, Tiffany created astonishingly compli-

[5] Robert Koch, *Louis C. Tiffany: Rebel in Glass* (New York: Crown Publishers, Inc., 1966 reissued ed.), 76.

17. Tiffany Glass and Decorating Company's pavilion in the Manufactures and Liberal Arts Building, from ground level showing *Feeding the Flamingos* window. Tiffany Studios study photograph. Morse Museum of American Art.

cated patterns and sub-patterns, finishes, and textures covering every surface of the ensemble with reflective material. The columns' mosaics involved four completely different, complex patterns, and the sixteen capitals also were of several different designs.

Tiffany relied heavily on the use of medieval decorative materials and ideas—especially on the metaphor of the church interior as the celestial city. In this concept the exterior is plain, even drab and generally unprepossessing, while the interior is transformed by color, proportion, and the careful manipulation of light into an entirely enveloping, "holistic," "celestial" experience. This concept of effectively transporting the worshiper from reality as we know it to another reality entirely—a reality of beauty and perfection—brings about the numinous experience Tiffany aimed to induce.

On entry one stands transfixed before a scene resplendent with ornament but tightly organized around a massive block of mosaic-covered marble raised up on a set of steps and surmounted by a series of concentric arches held in place by

glass-encrusted columns (fig. 18). The risers are decorated with liturgical phrases in Latin: first riser, "Holy, holy, holy, holy, holy"; second riser, "Our help is in the name of the Lord, who made heaven and earth"; third riser, "I will go to the altar of God, to God who gives joy to my youth."

The viewer's eyes are led up through the series of receding steps and platforms to the altar block. In *The "Lost" Treasures of Louis Comfort Tiffany*, Hugh McKean wrote: "The altar front is covered with one-fourth-inch squares of pearly-gray glass; some a little lighter than most; some a little darker. The variation gives it a cloudlike softness (fig. 19). Set in this quiet background are five circular devices. The central one contains the Alpha and Omega symbol of the Savior; those on either side the symbols of the four evangelists. All are executed in mother-of-pearl and glass sectiliae set

18. Above: Louis Comfort Tiffany. Tiffany Glass and Decorating Company. *Tiffany Chapel*, 1893, reassembled at Morse Museum of American Art, 1999. 37 x 24 ft. (12.1 x 7.9 m), 1,082 sq. ft., including baptistery.

19. Next page, top: Louis Comfort Tiffany. Tiffany Glass and Decorating Company. *Tiffany Chapel Altar*, 1893. Favrile glass mosaic, mother-of-pearl, and marble, 39 x 94 x 50 in. (99.1 x 238.8 x 127 cm). Morse Museum of American Art (75-023).

20. Next page, bottom: Center detail, *Tiffany Chapel Altar*.

in a background of pearly-white pebbles (fig. 20). The emphasis is on form. The materials are played against each other to underscore the beauty of each. St. Matthew's angel, St. Mark's lion, St. Luke's bull, and St. John's eagle are abstract designs, sophisticated enough to suit the intellectuals and understandable enough to suit the rest of us.

"The retable glows with a quotation from the scriptures done in tesserae in which gold leaf is sandwiched between a layer of opaque glass and a layer of clear [glass]. The door to the tabernacle has the exuberant ruggedness of Byzantine jewelry."[6]

Finally the viewer's eye discovers and settles for a moment in the geometric equilibrium of a focal point deep within the receding arches. The sumptuously colored glittering mosaic curved wall

called the reredos (fig. 21) above the altar is a mass of sectiliae cut from wrinkled, fractured, folded, lumpy, iridescent glass. Two peacocks, an ancient motif symbolizing eternity, face each other surrounded by a vine to symbolize the Eucharist. Above them a crown floats in a

[6] Hugh F. McKean, *The "Lost" Treasures of Louis Comfort Tiffany*, (Garden City, New York: Doubleday & Company, 1980, reissued Atglen, Pennsylvania: Shiffer Publishing, 2002), 136-137.

21. Louis Comfort Tiffany. Tiffany Glass and Decorating Company. *Tiffany Chapel Reredos*, ca. 1892. Favrile glass mosaic, 90 x 72 in. (228.6 x 182.9 cm). Morse Museum of American Art (U-075)

halo of beads, (fig. 22) their faceted surfaces creating a cloud of light. Under the crown seven large simulated amethysts have replaced the original garnets. A string of gilded beads is embedded in the plaster beneath, and glass hemispheres about one inch in diameter are set here and there throughout the design.

From the distant focus of the entry the arches and their supporting columns reach out gradually like great powerful arms, embracing the altar and filling the viewer's sight. The view is one of sumptuous color, symphonically mixed, mingled, and modulated in elaborately complex combinations of line, shade, hue, form, and material. Despite the chapel's unbelievable intricacy, it exerts a profound unified force that transports the visitor to some higher-than-human level of perception—a level on which pure beauty seems actually possible.

The concentric round arches that extend from the reredos outward form a partial dome that shelters the altar and links that mystically powerful space to a red barrel vault, which in turn links the entire altar and ciborium ensemble to the space of the faithful. The Latin inscription reads: "Holy, holy, holy, Lord God Almighty who was, who is, and who always will be."

To the right, connected to the altar area but distinguished from it by a screen formed by four columns surmounted by a decorative molding, is the baptistery (fig. 23). The centerpiece of this secondary space is the mosaic-covered baptismal font—a sphere resting on short columnar legs that emphasize its mass and geometric simplicity (fig. 24). The upper portion of the sphere is a dome made of hundreds of sectiliae cut in rhymthic patterns of glass, set in cames and backed with metal paint so the glass will function as a

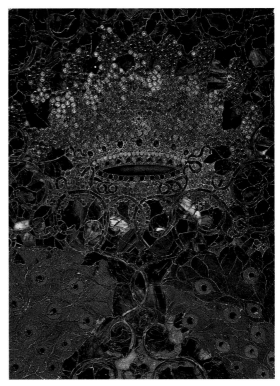

22. Detail, *Tiffany Chapel Reredos.*

mosaic. Without this it would transmit rather than reflect light like the lampshades Tiffany was shortly to begin to produce.

Forming a background to the font is a leaded window depicting a field of lilies viewed through three bays defined by the columns of a porch. The porch and columns are of a variegated colored glass that represent hard stone. Beyond this illusionary porch lies a heavenly field of luminescent lilies and the crown of a distant mountain—a brilliantly colored lush metaphor of Christ's innocence and innocence redeemed through baptism.

Above the viewer hangs a huge electrified light fixture, a metal structure in the form

23. Louis Comfort Tiffany. Tiffany Glass and Decorating Company. *Tiffany Chapel* baptistery, ca. 1892. Marble, Favrile glass and marble mosaic, and leaded Favrile glass, 12 ft. 6 in. x 9 ft. (4.1 x 2.9 m). Morse Museum of American Art.

24. Louis Comfort Tiffany. Tiffany Glass and Decorating Company. *Tiffany Chapel Baptismal Font*, ca. 1892. Marble, and Favrile glass and marble mosaic, 63 x diameter 42 in. (160 x 106.7 cm). Morse Museum of American Art (75-025:A&B).

25. Above: Louis Comfort Tiffany. Tiffany Glass and Decorating Company. *Tiffany Chapel Electrolier*, ca. 1892. Cast Favrile glass and metal, 120 x 96 in. (304.8 x 243.8 cm). Morse Museum of American Art (74-025:A&B).

26. Right: Louis Comfort Tiffany, Tiffany Glass and Decorating Company. *Tiffany Chapel Altar Cross*, ca. 1916, replacement of the original. Gilded plaster, gilded lead, Favrile glass and mother-of-pearl, 36 3/4 x 16 3/4 in. (93.3 x 42.5 cm). Morse Museum of American Art (75-016).

27. Next page: Louis Comfort Tiffany, Tiffany Glass and Decorating Company. *The Story of the Cross* window, ca. 1892. Leaded Favrile glass, diameter 104 1/2 in. (265.4 cm). Morse Museum of American Art (62-037).

of a three-dimensional cross (fig. 25), its eight-foot diameter cross pieces decorated with rectangular chunks of green glass and light bulbs that are calculated to produce a glowing dramatic sculpture rather than to actually light the chapel interior.

In contrast to the light effects of the altar ensemble—the electrified candlesticks and cross (fig. 26) designed to reflect light in a dim glow—the windows (fig. 27) are designed to emit light originating behind them. Though insufficient to light the chapel itself, these windows not only represent liturgical metaphors and religious narratives but produce color and atmosphere on the otherwise plain, dark, and colorless walls of the room. Like the altar, ciborium, and baptistery ensemble, they are geometrically simple but ornamentally complex, intricate, and colorful.

It was reported at the time that visitors to the chapel were so affected by religious emotion that men doffed their hats in response. Simultaneously, though, the chapel was a setting for liturgical costumes and ritual objects offered for sale by Tiffany's firm.

Also associated with the chapel were two additional great leaded windows, each depicting a religious theme while demonstrating Tiffany's stylistic range. The *Madonna and Child* (fig. 28) is in

Italian Renaissance style and was shorthanded at the time as the "Botticelli window" after the Italian Renaissance artist whose work was the main source for the window.[7] The other window, a lamentation, (fig. 29) is in Northern Renaissance style and also served as a vehicle for Louis Comfort Tiffany to present a portrait of his father whose face he used as the source of his depiction of Joseph of Aramathea.

In its time, Tiffany's chapel proved an astounding success with the general public, national leaders in design, and even the international design world which was not generally disposed to find merit in American art. Louis Comfort Tiffany's success was so great that at this time his career reached its zenith, and his reputation crossed the threshold into the ranks of the international design masters of the period. Following the fair, the chapel was disassembled, returned to Tiffany Glass and Decorating Company in New York, and apparently reassembled and shown to some unknown extent. It is said that Louis Comfort Tiffany let the Bethlehem Day Nursery collect a twenty-five-cent admission fee as a fund-raiser implying that access to the chapel was not general.

In any case, a wealthy woman, Mrs. Celia Whipple Wallace, bought the chapel for the Cathedral Church of Saint John the Divine under construction at the time in New York City.

28. Louis Comfort Tiffany. Tiffany Glass Company. *Madonna and Child* window, 1890. Leaded Favrile glass, diameter 84 in. (213.4 cm). Morse Museum of American Art (74-018).

Never placed as it was intended, the chapel was relegated to a basement crypt where its arches were cut to fit under a low, broadly vaulted ceiling. The original form of the chapel was completely changed, and major elements were placed in entirely different, generally unhappy locations, or omitted entirely.

By 1916 Mrs. Wallace, the donor, had died. A new church architect, Ralph Adams Cram, a committed follower of the Gothic style, had made it clear that the chapel's Neo-Byzantine style made

it unacceptable, and it would never again see the light of day. So Tiffany set out to rescue his great work, albeit in very poor condition, from the threat of oblivion and brought what remained to Laurelton Hall, the vast house he built for himself from 1902 to 1905 on Long Island (fig. 30).

By this time, the international Arts and Crafts Movement and the Aesthetic Movement, which had helped shape the taste that made Tiffany and his chapel a great success, had run their courses. Art Nouveau had passed by a decade before, and World War I was about to mark the real end of the nineteenth century and the beginning of the

[7] *Virgin and Child attended by Seven Angels*, Sandro Botticelli and assistants, 1482-85, Staatliche Museen, Berlin.

29. Louis Comfort Tiffany. Tiffany Glass and Decorating Company. *The Entombment* window, ca. 1892. Leaded Favrile glass, 104 x 73 in. (264.2 x 185.4 cm). Morse Museum of American Art (58-012).

machine age. The alliance of the machine, or perhaps more accurately collusion between the machine, design, and mass consumption, was well under way. The machine age saw the development of the electric forms of Art Deco and aerodynamically expressive streamlining—forerunners of the high-tech of today.

It wasn't until the 1960s when young designers, furniture makers, jewelry makers, glassblowers, and environmentalists revived some of the Arts and Crafts impulses of the late-nineteenth century that Tiffany's work began again to re-exert its power over the public. This revival of interest in Tiffany was encouraged by collectors such as the McKeans and advanced by scholars who began to reevaluate Tiffany's work.

But in 1916 when Tiffany carted his chapel back to his house—during the days of his waning reputation—he managed without public enthusiasm or support the first rescue of one of America's great interior spaces (fig. 31).

When he got the pieces to Laurelton Hall he remade parts that were destroyed by the Saint John installation and replaced the cross that had disappeared. But this installation was his and far more closely resembled the Chicago original than the Saint John version.

As fate would have it, the chapel trail still had not reached its end. Tiffany died in 1933, leaving his estate, including the chapel, to the foundation he created. But his trustees, to solve a financial dilemma in 1946, auctioned the contents of Laurelton Hall. Even that apparently didn't help

30. Top right: Louis Comfort Tiffany, designer. Robert Pryor, architect. Loggia entrance to Laurelton Hall, Oyster Bay, Long Island, New York, spring 1924. Morse Museum of American Art.

31. Right: Louis Comfort Tiffany. Tiffany Glass and Decorating Company/Tiffany Studios. Tiffany Chapel entrance on grounds of Laurelton Hall, Oyster Bay, Long Island, New York. Morse Museum of American Art.

32. Next page: Laurelton Hall during 1957 fire. *The New York Times.*

enough—the dispersal of the material Louis Comfort Tiffany most valued provided only temporary financial relief for the foundation. Later the estate was sold. By the late 1950s Laurelton Hall was empty of life; it is said it was used as storage for refrigerators. In any case, in 1957 it suffered a devastating fire (fig. 32) which left the house a ruin (fig. 33) though the chapel was spared. Following this, Tiffany's daughter Comfort (Mrs. Rodman Gilder) contacted Hugh McKean. She had heard Jeannette McKean had organized an exhibition of Tiffany work—an astonishingly prescient idea—at her gallery at Rollins College in Winter Park, Florida, and thought perhaps the McKeans would save a window.

Jeannette McKean visited the ruined site with her husband, Hugh McKean, and purchased all of the leaded windows and, later, remaining chapel parts, bringing them to Winter Park (fig. 34).

As years passed, Hugh and Jeannette McKean acquired the chapel furnishings that had been dispersed by the Tiffany Foundation and eventually assembled virtually all the elements Tiffany had installed at Laurelton Hall. This was the second rescue of Tiffany's great work.

Now the dream the McKeans had for the chapel, and certainly the hope Tiffany had to see his chapel survive, have been fulfilled with the cleaning and reassembling of the chapel elements at the Morse Museum. In April 1999 the Museum began to present the interior to the general public for all to enjoy for the first time since the 1893 fair.

The primary historical source that immediately comes to mind in connection with Tiffany's

Photograph Courtesy of *The New York Times*

Laurelton Hall During the Fire of 1957
At the center is the *Poppy Loggia*, now installed in the new American Wing of the Metropolitan Museum, New York.

chapel is certainly Byzantine architecture. One immediately thinks of the Hagia Sophia in Constantinople (537) and San Vitale in Ravenna (548) (fig. 35). Sumptuous decoration and dazzling mosaics cover nearly every square inch with linear patterns that form a kind of script or decorative calligraphy. Capitals are richly patterned, and the whole chapel is suffused with mystic light filtered through colored windows and reflected from surface to surface. These elements of Byzantine style Tiffany clearly embraced in his chapel.

The correspondence between mosaics Tiffany later created for the Wade Memorial Chapel (1901) in Cleveland, Ohio, clearly recalls the famous mosaics of Emperor Justinian and Empress Theodora at San Vitale.

Such a clear correspondence between a single Byzantine example and the chapel of 1893 has not emerged, but it is clear that the forms, colors, and materials Tiffany used obviously had sources in Byzantine church architecture. Doubtless scholars will elaborate on these and other sources perhaps including Islamic and Celtic art and further illumi-

34. Hugh F. McKean standing on ruins of Laurelton Hall, 1957. Archival photograph, Morse Museum of American Art.

nate Tiffany's use of such sources in due course.

Exerting awesome control over his incredibly rich historical sources, complex materials, powerful forms, and intricate surface patterns, Tiffany created additional allusions over and above those to Byzantium, the Middle Ages, and the obvious allusions to God and religion inherent in the nature of a chapel.

While Louis Comfort Tiffany was in many ways distinctively American and his art was distinctly American, he did not achieve the artistic status he enjoyed in the 1890s in New York and in Europe without taking into account leading developments in European art. In connection with the chapel this meant Aestheticism and the style or movement called Symbolism.

Certainly an important segment of the chapel's audience would not only have been aware of Symbolist painting but would have shared to some extent at least Symbolist ideas and the outlook of Aestheticism in general.

On a philosophical level, the Aesthetes gave the same high status to beauty that Tiffany is well known to have assigned it. In this view, artistic beauty is held in such high regard that it is beyond

33. Laurelton Hall following 1957 fire. Archival photograph, Morse Museum of American Art.

religious concepts and beliefs at the same time that it is higher too than science and logic. In fact, among the most committed Aesthetes, art was the chosen refuge from a perceived inadequacy of religion or science to explain the world.

Such a position would have been, one imagines, the background to the statement Tiffany has been said to have made[8] that his was a chapel in which to worship art.

Even, however, if to portray Tiffany as an Aesthete is not fully explanatory, certainly the cultivated northeastern American audience was not without a strain of this point of view.

And the cultivated European audience, particularly the French, could not have seen the chapel or experienced it through chromolithographs or even through reports by fellow countrymen without drawing on their experience of such literature as Huysmans' *A Rebours*[9] or the paintings of Gustave Moreau (1826-1898).

One of the key individuals in the establishment of the international aspect of Tiffany's grand reputation was Siegfried Bing, founder of the famous shop L'Art Nouveau and purveyor of Tiffany glass to Europeans.

Surely Bing would have seen the capacity of Tiffany's chapel to bear the enthusiastic interpretation of French Aesthetes and thereby raise Tiffany's achievement from the category of ecclesiastical architecture to the broader context of art in a time when art trumped both science and religion for a good many artists, intellectuals, thinkers, and tastemakers.

The visual side of this view rests on the related light, color, atmospheric, and even, in a general way, thematic aspects of pictures such as Moreau's famous *Apparition* and Tiffany's chapel.

Moreau, like other Symbolists, transports us to an exotic otherworldly and mystical location set in a church-like building suggestive by color, light, and patterned decoration of Byzantium. In *Apparition*, we witness a vision so surreal and sumptuous that its primary aim seems to be to induce exaggerated sensations that are not part of ordinary experience and not a part of conventional religions either.

However one feels about this issue of the sociability among contemporaneous French painting, Aestheticism, and Tiffany's chapel, the chapel encourages and rewards a wide variety of interpretations. These range from the simple level of beautiful, useful religious object to avant-garde pure art-for-art's-sake. This capacity is one indicator of the chapel's greatness and reason for its universal appeal both in 1893 and now a century later. After all, the capacity of any object to reasonably accommodate many, including even contradictory, interpretations is one of the necessary conditions of its being a masterpiece and crucial to its attracting keen interest in very different times and very different places.

35. Detail, *The Call of Peter and Andrew*, San Vitale, Ravenna, Italy, 548. Mosaic.

[8] Tessa Paul, *The Art of Louis Comfort Tiffany* (New York and Avenel, N.J.: Crescent Books, 1992), 61.

[9] J.K. Huysmans, *Against the Grain (A Rebours)*, (New York: Dover Publications, 1969). The novel was first published in 1884.

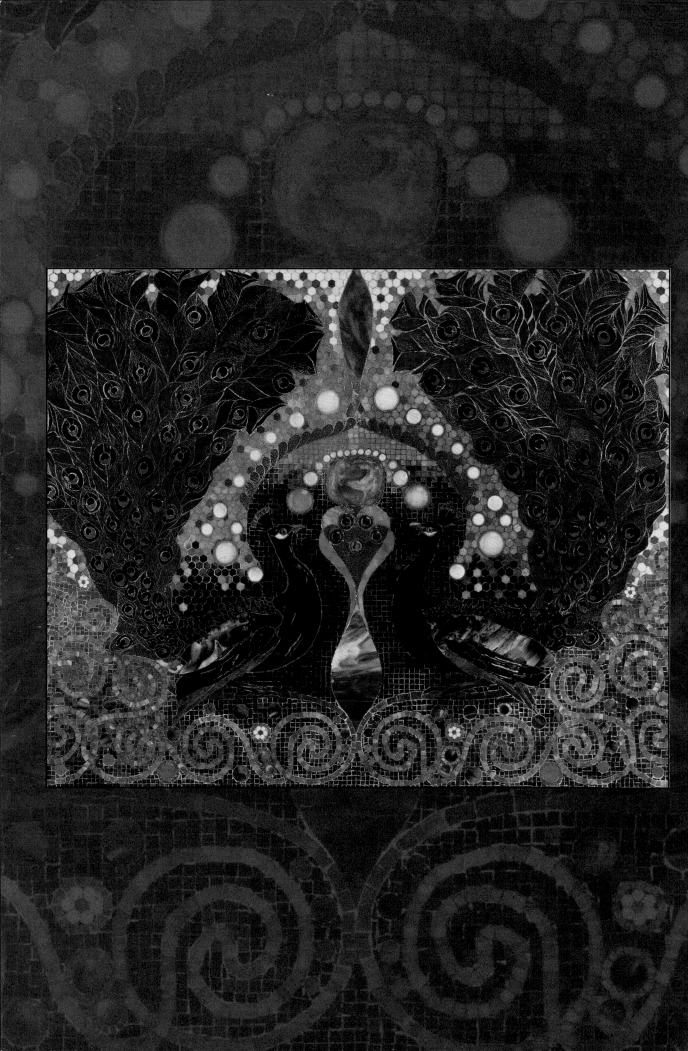

Louis C. Tiffany and the
DAWNING OF A NEW ERA FOR MOSAICS

by ALICE COONEY FRELINGHUYSEN

The chapel Louis Comfort Tiffany designed and had executed under his direction in his workrooms for display at the 1893 World's Columbian Exposition had a significant impact on his visibility and subsequently the direction of his career. Glass and marble mosaic form the core of the chapel's decorative program. Indeed, Tiffany utilized mosaics in his decorative schemes to a far greater extent than has been traditionally recognized, incorporating them into the earliest of his decorative work.

One reason for the lack of attention given to this branch of the arts of Tiffany may be that mosaics were primarily intended for use in interior decoration, and many of those interiors either no longer survive today, or are contained in public buildings and churches. Additionally, they have received little attention in the marketplace, except for a few small-scale decorative panels that have been purchased by collectors or museums. It is worth examining, therefore, the development of Tiffany's work in mosaic as it led up to the 1893 chapel, and also taking a closer look at the influence that this exhibition had on subsequent mosaics.

In 1896 the Tiffany Glass and Decorating Company published an entire pamphlet devoted to Mosaics, underscoring the importance the firm placed on this aspect of its decorative work.[1] The pamphlet extolled the traditional uses of mosaic decoration from ancient times through the Byzantine era up to 1308, and its subsequent revival in Venice in the mid-nineteenth century. It continued with a discourse on the contribution to the art made by Louis C. Tiffany, beginning in 1879, and through subsequent decades when he incorporated it for all manner of decoration, employing it "wherever he could, endeavoring to make manifest to all its color-decorative possibilities."[2]

---

[1] Tiffany Glass and Decorating Company, *Mosaic Glass for Walls, Ceilings, Inlays and Other Ornamental Work* (New York, 1896). Collection of The Metropolitan Museum of Art.

[2] Ibid, 14.

The important role mosaic decoration played in architectural decoration dates to ancient times. Stone mosaic covered the floors and glass mosaic the walls of the homes of the highest classes in ancient Roman times, most notably those at Herculaneum and Pompeii. Mosaic decoration was then richly embraced during the twelfth and thirteenth centuries, especially as it provided rich adornment to churches and palaces, notably at Palermo and Monreale in Sicily, San Vitale in Ravenna, and Hagia Sophia in Constantinople. By the fifteenth century, however, classic wall mosaic had virtually disappeared as an architectural art form. When the Gothic Revival took place in England beginning in the 1830s, first with the work of Pugin and later with other medieval revivalists, initially few artists embraced mosaic work. Yet the second half of the nineteenth century saw a renewed interest in mosaics with the establishment in England in 1850 of a mosaics workshop at the South Kensington Museum and in the work of Edward Burne-Jones and Henry Richmond. Salviati, a Venetian firm that worked in England, had produced the mosaics for St. Paul's Cathedral in London after cartoons by Alfred Stevens and Frederick Watts. Charles Locke Eastlake cited Salviati's mosaics in his *Hints on Household Taste*, first published in England in 1862. In his book, which had numerous printings in America beginning in 1868, Eastlake wrote that mosaics had "advantages in mural decoration over fresco, in such climate as that of England."[3] Yet, mosaic work did not keep pace with the other decorative arts until American artists, notably Louis Comfort Tiffany, expanded its function and decorative possibilities in ways hitherto unknown.

Tiffany was not the only American artist to exploit the ornamental properties of mosaic. Christian Herter, a preeminent cabinetmaker and decorator, and Tiffany's most significant competition in New York, utilized it for the first time in 1882 in the grand mansion being built by William H. Vanderbilt at Fifth Avenue and 57th Street.[4] The Vanderbilt commission was publicly heralded as the first major use of the medium in America. In the late 1880s, the Herter firm lavishly applied mosaic decoration, primarily composed of stone tesserae, for the sumptuous bathroom of the Robert Garrett house in Baltimore, Maryland.[5] Enormous dolphins, each with a child on his back, all on a rich gold background, were displayed on facing walls. By the end of the decade, there were some eight firms, including Tiffany's, in New York City alone which considered the fabrication of mosaics all or part of their business. In total they employed some fifty mosaic workers.[6]

Tiffany's interest in mosaic decoration was kindled, no doubt, by mosaic work he saw during his many travels abroad. He went to Sicily in 1865-66, and while there must certainly have seen the impressive Norman mosaic work in Palermo and Monreale. On more than one occasion, his travels took him to Italy, and it is likely that Ravenna, home to the great mosaics of San Vitale, was on his itinerary. In Venice he would have visited San Marco and witnessed the extensive mosaic decoration there. The decorative possibilities of mosaics complemented Tiffany's abiding interest in elaborated architecture and in wall and floor surfaces, and he often explored new materials for

3 Charles Locke Eastlake, *Hints on Household Taste* (Boston: James R. Osgood and Company, 1872), 254.

4 For information on Herter Brothers' decoration of the William H. Vanderbilt house, see Katherine S. Howe, Alice Cooney Frelinghuysen, et. al., *Herter Brothers: Furniture and Interiors for a Gilded Age* (New York: Abrams, 1993), 200-11.

5 See Susan Gerwe Tripp, "Evergreen House, Baltimore, Maryland," *Antiques Magazine*, Vol. 139, No. 2 (February 1991), 388-97.

6 "Mosaics in Interior Decoration," *Art Amateur*, Vol. 22 (April 1890), 104-105.

their ornamentation. More importantly, mosaics embraced his interest in decorative surfaces with glass, which early on became his primary focus.

One of the most appealing characteristics of mosaics was its purported durability, and consequently its sense of permanence. Its colors would not fade or wear, and it would hold its beauty over time. In the small publication that Tiffany's firm produced in 1896, devoted exclusively to mosaics, the durability of the material was especially noted. It "would resist effectually the corrosion of natural and artificial decay, ones that would hold their pristine beauty the longest…. It is non-absorbant, fireproof, and practically indestructible except by direct violence."[7] The practical properties of mosaic glass as its essential ingredient, and its application to wall and floor surfaces, combined to make the medium, for Tiffany, highly desirable as a decorative component in the earliest of his interiors.

Tiffany claimed that his initial foray into mosaics occurred as part of the designs he executed for the Union League Club in 1879. In that year, he joined rival designers John La Farge and Cottier & Company, both of New York, and Frank Hill Smith of Boston to decorate a new building for the prestigious men's club at Fifth Avenue and 39th Street. (The building and its decorations no longer survive.) Tiffany's role was to decorate the main hall and the stairways. The mosaics he incorporated into the

scheme reinforced the theme of reflective and iridescent surfaces already found in Tiffany's wall decoration of the hallway, embellished "with small triangles of silver leaf, and which have an Oriental effect."[8] The last details of decoration provided by Tiffany were two round mosaics that ornamented the walls above the upper flight of stairs where the stairway bifurcated to ascend to the second floor. Contrary to Tiffany's claim that the mosaics dated to 1879, they were not actually installed until 1881 or 1882. They were described in 1881, just prior to their installation, and their subject, one that would recur in Tiffany's mosaic work later in his career, was noted: "peacocks treated in the Venetian manner with glass mosaic."[9]

Tiffany made numerous experiments in glass in the early 1880s. Some of these experiments which resulted in patent applications involved an exploration of the use of glass for mosaic or mosaic-like decoration. In 1881, for example, he registered a patent for the "insertion of such glass among other pieces of colored glass in a window or mosaic."[10] In that same year, Tiffany founded one of several partnerships that he would undertake in his early career, this new company called Louis C. Tiffany & Co., Associated Artists (formerly Wheeler & Tiffany).[11] In an early published description of the firm's scope it was noted that the work for interiors included mural decoration, "designs for the decorative use of wood and metals in interior and cabinet work; [and] embroidery fabrics." Special mention was made of "the making and arrangement of tinted and colored glass mosaic."[12]

Prior to the 1893 chapel, Tiffany utilized mosaic in a number of important domestic interiors. In 1881, Cornelius Vanderbilt II approved designs suggested by Tiffany for interior spaces of the grand new residence designed by George B. Post at Fifth Avenue

7   Tiffany Glass and Decorating Company. *Glass Mosaic* (1896), 15.

8   "The Architectural Progress of New York City," *Frank Leslie's Popular Monthly*, Vol. 15 (April 1883), 387.

9   The mosaics were not quite finished when the building opened, and tapestries were hung to conceal their placement until their completion. "A New Palace," (1881), 8. Unidentified photo copy in departmental files, American Decorative Arts, The Metropolitan Museum of Art.

10 United States Patent No. 237416. February 8, 1881. United States Department of Commerce, Patent and Trademark Office, Washington, D.C.

11 Roberta A. Mayer and Carolyn K. Lane, "Disassociating the Associated Artists: The Early Business Ventures of Louis C. Tiffany, Candace T. Wheeler, and Lockwood de Forest," *Bard Graduate Center Studies in the Decorative Arts*, Vol. VIII, no. 2 (Spring-Summer 2001), 2-36.

12 "Louis C. Tiffany & Co.—Associated Artists, I," *Harper's Bazaar*, Vol. 14 (July 23, 1881), 471.

and 57th Street. Like the Union League Club, several preeminent decorators were involved in the Vanderbilt project. Tiffany's principal competitor, John La Farge, was commissioned for a number of the windows and decorations, while Tiffany's associate Candace Wheeler provided numerous textiles for the house. His own primary contribution was for the sumptuous drawing room on the first floor. It was his introduction of mosaic into the scheme that drew particular attention, prompting one observer to cite it as "another experimental departure" for the artist.[13] The discovery of several letters written by Duncan Gay, a young artist who worked for Tiffany in the early 1880s and whose sister would later become Tiffany's leading artisan working in enamelwork, sheds additional light on the Vanderbilt mosaics. In March of 1883, Gay, while working with Tiffany in St. Augustine, Florida, acknowledged that "Mr. Vanderbilt's mosaic is very nice work but it is terrible slow."[14] In a letter written only four days later, Gay said his work on the Vanderbilt project was almost complete, and that "I think I shall ship it to New York this week."[15] That the mosaic could be fabricated in Florida, while Tiffany was vacationing with his family, and then shipped to New York seems somewhat implausible, but it was actually composed of small panels of glass mosaic, and then when installed in the ceiling, bordered by "demarcations of woodwork in geometrical designs."[16] The glass was described as ancient glass from Thebes, Pompeii, and Cyprus, with the characteristic iridescent surface resulting from being long buried in the earth. Little mention was made of the design, making it difficult to conjure up a clear image as described: "...the scintillant bits are arranged in butterflies, orchids, and other delicate forms."[17] Although the dining room has long since been destroyed, one

contemporary account extolled the iridescent glass ceiling, which gave "a splendid effect at night."[18]

In 1885, two years after the completion of Tiffany's contribution to the Vanderbilt commission, Louis's father, Charles, commissioned McKim, Mead and White to design a large Romanesque Revival structure at 72nd Street and Madison Avenue. It was intended to be a multi-family dwelling house with Charles occupying the first two floors, his daughter, the third floor, and Louis, with his wife and children, the fourth and top floors. Tiffany's designs for his own apartment were among the most exotic and innovative of his career. They heralded a design scheme that was bursting with objects of art from China, Japan, Persia, and India, and it abounded in unusual materials and irregularities of decoration, floor levels, and even ceilings, which were variously curved or vaulted. Shortly after it was completed, it was described as "unique" and as "an aesthetic warehouse."[19] It was also another early example in which Tiffany prominently incorporated decorative glass mosaic into the ornamentation of a domestic interior, this time for himself. In the library, for example, in addition to leaded-glass windows of magnolia branches and walls embellished with *tsuba*, or Japanese sword guards, one wall with the rounded top of the oriel it occupied was inlaid with "deep blue glass mosaics studded with jewels which sparkle in the dull light of day, and which at night must be resplendent above the pendant

13 "New York City Building Items," *The Manufacturer and Builder*, Vol. 14 (April 1882), 90.

14 Letter from Duncan Gay to his mother, St. Augustine, Florida, March 16, 1883. Courtesy of Duncan Gay's daughter, Suzanne Gay Linville, and her son, Jim Linville.

15 Duncan Gay to his mother, St. Augustine, Florida, March 20, 1883. Courtesy of Gay's daughter, Suzanne Gay Linville, and her son, Jim Linville.

16 "New York City Building Items," *The Manufacturer and Builder*, Vol. 14 (April 1882), 90.

17 "The Architectural Process of New York City," *Frank Leslie's Popular Monthly*, Vol. 15 (April 1883), 385.

18 Ibid.

19 Mary Gay Humphreys, "Bits in the Tiffany House," *Art Amateur*, Vol. 16, no. 2 (1887), 40.

gas-light."[20] From the following year on, in 1886, the Tiffany Glass Company, as it had been called since 1885, consistently advertised glass mosaic in addition to stained-glass windows and other decorations.[21]

Tiffany's own home and the Vanderbilt mansion laid the groundwork for what was arguably the zenith of Tiffany's use of mosaics for a domestic interior, the New York house of two of the artist's most ardent and sympathetic patrons, Louisine and Henry Osborne Havemeyer. Unlike the Vanderbilt mansion to which Tiffany contributed portions of the decorative scheme, the Havemeyer project allowed Tiffany,

along with his colleague the American painter Samuel Colman, to decorate every aspect of the unusual house. In this instance, the clients had enormous confidence in Tiffany's work, and the sober and conservative exterior in the Romanesque Revival style designed by Charles Coolidge Haight could not prepare the visitor for the avant-garde splendors that lay within. Glass was utilized in leaded-glass windows and lighting fixtures, but its use as mosaic decoration became the signature element of the house. This was seen to great effect in the entrance hall (fig. 36). The semi-public function of the hall made it eminently suitable for a generous use of mosaic. In itself it conveyed an imposing grandeur, further enhanced by the architectural reference of the main stairway to the Doges Palace in Venice. Every inch of surface area was

36. Entrance hall of H.O. Havemeyer House, by Louis C. Tiffany, 1 East 66th Street, New York City, completed 1892. Archival photograph, The Metropolitan Museum of Art.

utilized for decorative mosaics. The floor was embedded with over one million Hispano-Moresque tiles, and the walls were completely covered in glass mosaic ornament. They were divided into rectangular sections filled with subtle shades of opalescent, green, and gold glass surrounded by more colorful decorative borders in a geometric pattern. A deep frieze encircled the room, composed of repeated mosaic panels. Islamic motifs inspired the design, which featured stylized plant motifs emanating from golden scrolls on a rich deep blue ground (fig. 37). Siegfried Bing, the noted Parisian dealer who promoted Tiffany's work extensively in Europe and whose gallery was called L'Art Nouveau, made particular note of the mosaics in the Havemeyers' house after he visited America in 1894 saying, "From the walls of spacious entrance halls, gleamed a rich variety of subtle shadings, sober, chalky whites surmounted by polychromed friezes, diapered with the thousand details of woven cashmere."[22]

The dazzling focal point of the shimmering entrance hall was the overmantel glass mosaic depicting two peacocks arranged symmetrically and framed by golden scrolls that complemented the frieze panels (fig. 38). The opulently hued and patterned peacock was a motif especially appropriate to the mosaic medium and one first used by Tiffany in his decorations for the Union League Club. It had become a favorite of late-nineteenth-century artists because of its potent many-leveled symbolism. Nothing could replicate better the oily sheen of the bird's feathers, however, than Tiffany's signature iridescent glass. The use of the motif recalls the exotic and highly controversial "Peacock Room," the dining room commissioned by Sir Frederick Leyland from James Abbott McNeil Whistler, of 1876–77. On the other hand, the subject and medium suggest

37. Mosaic panel from frieze in H.O. Havemeyer House. Louis Comfort Tiffany. *Pavonine Mosaic Frieze*, 1890-91, iridescent glass and plaster. University of Michigan School of Art and College of Architecture and Urban Planning, on extended loan to the University of Michigan Museum of Art. (1986.146.8A). Photograph by Patrick Young.

that the Havemeyer entrance hall may be more closely linked to the main hall of Lord Leighton's house in London, finished in 1880.[23] The peacock overmantel, however, has particular significance in the context of this publication in that it was the inspiration for the peacock mosaic reredos for the chapel Tiffany executed for the World's Columbian Exposition in Chicago only a few years later (see fig. 21). When one compares the two, it becomes clear that the proportions of the peacocks remain identical—as if taken from the same working cartoon. Yet, Tiffany extended the height of the mosaic by double in the Chicago version where jewel-like

20 Ibid., 42.

21 Advertisement in July 17, 1886, by the Tiffany Glass Company. *Art Interchange*, Vol. 17 (July 17, 1886).

22 S. Bing, "Artistic America," trans. of the 1895 French version, "La Culture artistique en Amérique," by Benita Eisler, in *Artistic America, Tiffany Glass, and Art Nouveau*, intro. Robert Koch (Cambridge, Mass., and London, 1970), 130.

23 For information and illustration of Leighton's Arab Hall, see Tim Barringer and Elizabeth Prettejohn, eds., *Frederic Leighton: Antiquity, Renaissance, Modernity* (New Haven & London: Yale University Press, Studies in British Art 5, 1999).

heavens above were added, and surmounted by a resplendent glass jewel-encrusted crown of God.

Indeed, mosaic decoration seemed especially suited to ecclesiastic decoration. The period of the 1880s was one of tremendous growth both culturally and economically for the country. The economic prosperity in the post Civil War years contributed greatly to the building boom of churches, over 1,000 of which were at one stage or another of construction by 1888. The services of decorating firms like Tiffany's

were required to furnish these often grand houses of worship with wall decoration, leaded-glass windows, flooring, furniture, silver chalices, vestments, and mosaic. Tiffany's full-service firm could provide a complete decorative scheme, or the church or a parishioner might commission Tiffany's firm to create only one element to be incorporated into a larger whole.

One of the earliest, and most unusual, churches for which Tiffany's ateliers provided the entire decorative program—and one of the first uses by Tiffany of mosaics in an ecclesiastic setting—was St. Hubert's Chapel, in what is now Kinnelon, New Jersey. Kinnelon was a five-thousand-acre tract of land on which Francis S. Kinney, a tobacco magnate, built his

38. Overmantel mosaic in H.O. Havemeyer House. Louis Comfort Tiffany. *Peacock Mosaic*, 1890-91, cabochon glass and plaster. University of Michigan School of Art and College of Architecture and Urban Planning, on extended loan to the University of Michigan Museum of Art. (1986.146.9). Photograph by Patrick Young.

country estate, complete with a working farm and hunting and fishing preserves. In addition, Kinney built a small private chapel for his wife, Francis, located on a tiny island in the center of Lake Kinnelon. Although conceived in the spring of 1886, it would be another three and a half years until it was consecrated. The theme of the chapel was dedicated to St. Hubert, who, appropriately, given Kinney's interests, was a master huntsman. Mosaics feature prominently in the interior decoration, furnished by Tiffany's firm, which also provided the windows and sculptural reliefs in bronze. The mosaic utilized throughout the chapel, however, is not just glass, like many of the domestic interiors discussed, but also is composed of marble and other colored stones. The mosaic floor was said to have consisted of three hundred thousand pieces of marble, in patterns modeled on thirteenth-century designs. It features birds and grapes, of salmon, green, and tan stone. Mosaic continues, this time of glass and glass jewels in combination with marble, on the altar. When one looks at the St. Hubert's altar, one can immediately extrapolate to the glass and marble mosaic of the World's Columbian Exposition chapel of a few years later. Typical of Tiffany's interest in creating a unified interior, the designs of the mosaics on the floor and altar are again referenced in the leaded-glass windows, and even in the exotic hanging light fixture. The sumptuousness of the mosaics contrasts sharply with the rough-hewn stone of the rustic interior walls.

The St. Hubert's commission laid the groundwork upon which numerous churches would be designed during the ensuing decade, demonstrating Tiffany's strong predelection for glass and stone mosaic, the culmination of which was the exhibi-

tion chapel for the 1893 Chicago world's fair. Mosaic decoration already had played a role at the World's Columbian Exposition in Chicago of 1893 in the Columbus Memorial Building which displayed two glass mosaic panels illustrating Columbus's discovery of America. These mosaics were said to have been produced by the Company Murano. Yet Tiffany's chapel surpassed the traditional use of mosaic decoration.[24]

One aspect of the mosaic decoration for the Tiffany chapel was borrowed from historical use whereby mosaic was inlaid in marble columns, stairways, and other parts of the interior architecture of a building. Historically, shallow recesses were chiseled in the face of the marble in outline designs, and then filled with glass tesserae of various colors.[25] Tiffany enlivened his chapel's plain rectangular white marble altar with mosaic patterns in shimmering Favrile glass tesserae and jewels, as well as mother-of-pearl, quartz pebbles, and copper beads. The chapel's baptismal font features a complex patterning of the same. Mosaic even decorates the stair risers. Behind the altar, the towering reredos is a resplendant mosaic of a pair of peacocks in full plumage set into undulating scrolls (borrowed from the Havemeyer mosaic) and surmounted by a jeweled crown of the spiritual heavens.

One cannot overstate the impact that the success of Tiffany's exhibition at the Chicago World's Columbian Exposition, and especially his chapel, replete with mosaic decoration, had on his subsequent work. Among the nearly one and one-half million individuals who viewed the chapel were

[24] Sharon Darling, *Chicago Ceramics & Glass* (Chicago: Chicago Historical Society, 1979), 137.

[25] See W. H. Thomas, "Glass Mosaic—An Old Art with a New Distinction," *The International Studio*, vol. 28 (1906), 72-78.

those who were contemplating various building projects, in which they wished to lavish the grandeur and luster that mosaic decoration conveyed. Numerous commissions for decorations in mosaic, primarily for public buildings or churches, many in Chicago, followed on the heels of the 1893 fair, presumably as a direct consequence of it.

One such admirer was Mrs. Henry Field, the widow of Henry Field, brother of dry-goods magnate Marshall Field. In 1893, Mrs. Field asked Tiffany to design a gallery in her husband's memory for the Art Institute of Chicago. She had requested that the gallery be designed as an exhibition space for the couple's collection of nineteenth-century French paintings and that it be a reflection of the room in which they had hung in her own home. When it opened to the public in 1894, *The Chicago Tribune* praised its sophisticated and skillful design. Although subtle in its overall effect, mosaic played a significant part in the decoration. The room, known today only through the newspaper descriptions of it, an archival photograph, and a surviving drawing of one elevation (fig. 39), was sumptuous in its use of materials, but at the same time the overall effect was understated. The gallery displayed a mosaic floor in soft tones of green, yellow, red, pale pink, and black stone. The fireplace, the only focal point other than the pictures, was flanked by ebony pilasters with jeweled bronze caps—two to a side—supporting an ebony canopy edged with pale yellow and emerald green glass

39. Louis Comfort Tiffany. Tiffany Glass and Decorating Company. *Design for Henry Field Memorial Gallery at the Art Institute of Chicago,* ca. 1893-94. Watercolor on paper, 20 x 13 in. (51.4 x 34.9 cm). The Metropolitan Museum of Art, Purchase, Walter Hoving and Julia T. Weld Gifts and Dodge Fund, 1967 (67.654.4).

40. Jacob Holzer, Tiffany Glass and Decorating Company. *Joliet and the Chief of the Illinois Tribe*. Mosaic frieze panel in Marquette Building, Chicago, completed 1895. Photograph by Hedrich Blessing.

tesserae. The entire fireplace was surrounded by a mosaic of golden bronze colored glass. All of the woodwork was of highly polished ebony, and the door casings and panels were inset with tiny squares of mother-of-pearl. The dado was particularly unusual, faced with mosaic that shaded subtly from grays and bronze browns to black, the predominant color. The frieze, stenciled in metallic colors in a geometric pattern, echoed the mosaic designs elsewhere in the room.[26]

One of the most ambitious commissions that followed the 1893 world's fair in Chicago was the mosaic frieze that completely encircled the first floor hall or rotunda in what can be considered one of the new multi-storied skyscraper office buildings. The building, completed in 1895, was designed by the noted Chicago architectural firm of Holabird & Roche. This semi-public space features nine panels four feet high, some as large as fifteen feet wide, commemorating the famous expedition of Louis Joliet and Jacques Marquette, and their exploration from Lake Michigan and down the Mississippi River. Three narrative scenes depict incidents that occurred during the expedition: the priest Marquette blessing the boat; Joliet and the chief of the Illinois tribe; and the death of Marquette. The figures are set

frieze-like within landscape settings and reveal a strong illustrative character (fig. 40). The details of the trees, grass, and figures are realized in glass with extraordinary verisimilitude. The rendering of the spring foliage drew special comment from period newspaper accounts. Three other panels alternate with the narrative scenes and are more decorative (fig. 41), featuring portraits of Marquette, Joliet, and the Indian chief, within roundels depicted as if suspended like medals. The central portraits are flanked by two trophies, each composed of attributes appropriate to the individual represented. For example, suits of armor and various weapons compose the trophies flanking Joliet, and religious attributes on one side and a paddle, peace pipes, and other implements of the voyage flank the portrait of Marquette. Particularly effective in their use are large shaped pieces of glass of various colors, as seen for example in the replication of the canoe paddle, complete with the simulation of wood grain. Each tooth, claw, or bead was cut to the actual shape and incorporated as part of the overall composition. The trophies are suspended from a swag of an Indian textile in a geometric pattern, intricately carried out in tiny tesserae. The background of these decorative panels is created of irregular horizontal bands of blue and green glass that are subtly shaded from pale blue at the top, blue and green in the middle, and deep blue at the bottom. The

[26] "For the Field Gems: Arrangements for the Barbazon [sic] Pictures in the Institute," *The Chicago Tribune*, August 12, 1894.

41. Mosaic frieze panel in Marquette Building. Photograph by Hedrich Blessing.

mosaics were executed in Tiffany's workshops using countless permutations of his glass, a tour de force of Tiffany's mosaic oeuvre. Yet the frieze's design is credited to the artist Jacob Adolph Holzer (1858-1938), who was working for Tiffany at the time. Perhaps due to Holzer's influence, it was decidedly literal and narrative in contrast to the majority of Tiffany's work in mosaics which was far more stylized, geometric, and ultimately more decorative in appearance, as exemplified by the Chicago Public Library of the following year, also designed by Holzer.

Jacob Adolph Holzer, a Swiss artist who began working for Tiffany about 1886, was the primary artist for Tiffany's mosaics. He had studied in Paris with painters and decorators Louis-Edouard Fournier and Paul-Albert Besnard, before emigrating to the United States in 1875.[27] He initially studied and worked with Augustus Saint Gaudens and John La Farge. His most important work prior to his involvement with Tiffany was the decorative embellishments which included windows, bronze relief panels, stained glass, and mosaics, for the vestibule of The Osborne apartment house in New York in 1885. One critic described the apartment a few years after its completion, saying, "The main

entrance is said to be the finest in New York, with heavy oaken doors, rare marbles, mosaic, frescoes and stained glass."[28] Holzer rose swiftly at Tiffany's, becoming the chief designer and art director for the Tiffany Glass Company in 1890, a post he held until 1896, during which period some of the firm's most significant work in mosaics was completed.

Among Holzer's most complex mosaic designs were those for the Chicago Public Library (now the Chicago Cultural Center). The building was designed by Charles Coolidge, who maintained the Chicago arm of the Boston firm Shepley, Rutan & Coolidge. The sumptuous mosaic decoration that encrusted the dome, delivery room, and stairway complemented the grandeur and large scale of the architectural spaces.[29] The grand stairway was described in the *Mosaics* pamphlet published by Tiffany Glass and Decorating Company just after this commission was completed: "of white Italian veined marble…inlaid with a combination of glass mosaic with Royal Irish green marble and pearl."[30] The predominant color scheme, selected by Holzer, consisted of the various cool whites of the marble, with the architectural details delineated and embellished on every surface with infinite variations of geometric patterns in colors of green,

[27] For more information on Holzer, and especially his work and collecting after he returned to Europe, see Marie-Dominique Sanchez and Edda Guglielmetti, "Jacob-Adolphe Holzer (1858-1938)," *L'Art d'imiter: Images de la Reanissance italienne au Musée d'art et d'histoire,* ed. Mauro Natale and Claude Ritschard (Genève: Département des affaire culturelles, 1999), 310-26.

[28] *Illustrated New York: the Metropolis of Today* (New York, 1888), 75.

[29] The library, located at Michigan Avenue and Washington Street, has been preserved and is now the Chicago Cultural Center.

[30] Tiffany Glass and Decorating Company, *Glass Mosaic,* 22.

42. Jacob Holzer, Tiffany Glass and Decorating Company. Mosaic work in the grand staircase of the Chicago Public Library (now the Chicago Cultural Center), completed 1896. Photograph by Hedrich Blessing.

blue, and gold. The grand staircase featured a dome decorated with dense Renaissance scrollwork designs, and the wall surfaces, delineated as paneling, were picked out in cosmatesque designs (fig. 42). In what was originally the delivery room, rectangular reserves enclosed the names of great historical philosophers and writers, and larger tablets paid homage to significant figures in the history of libraries. In one final panel, a candelabrum symbolic of the light of knowledge, was surmounted by an open book, and the whole was enclosed in a scrolled cartouche and wreath. The date of the completion of the library—1896—was depicted in mosaic Roman numerals below. At the time of its completion, the Chicago Public Library was considered, "by far the most extensive piece of wall-mosaic work undertaken since the decoration of the Cathedral, at Monreale, Sicily, in the 13th c."[31]

The 1893 exposition chapel, however, most compellingly demonstrated the range of decorations that Tiffany's workshops could provide for synagogues and churches of all denominations. At the same time, it illustrated the totality of the firm's work and its ability to execute an entire project of unity of character and design. As a result, shortly after the exposition, many churches took advantage of these services to decorate newly built structures or to redecorate existing buildings. Closer to the firm's headquarters, there are several noted examples of its work in New York State. Among the most notable decorations are those executed during the mid- to late-1890s, the period of Tiffany's most important work.

The Willard Memorial Chapel built between 1892 and 1894 in Auburn, New York, is a small gem of an ecclesiastic building where mosaic decoration is interspersed throughout the integrated interior. The floor is completely covered in stone mosaic in shades of tan, salmon, and green, recalling the color scheme that Tiffany had used earlier for the floor at St. Hubert's Chapel. The windows are mosaic-like due to their geometric design, muted palette, and the relatively small size of the individual pieces of glass. In addition to the floor, however, mosaic decoration takes the form of exotic ornament on the pulpit. The center back panel features geometric patterning based on thirteenth-century designs. The sides were equally elaborately ornamented in carved leafy decoration. In addition, at the back of the nave is an unusual glass and gilded plaster relief depicting the allegorical figures of Faith, Hope, and Charity in the style of the American Renaissance, by Holzer, the artist who signed it. The walls of the chapel, although neutral in color today and known only through one surviving black and white photograph of the interior

[31] Ibid, 22.

before it was redone sometime in this century, were originally painted under Tiffany's direction in a geometric pattern reminiscent of mosaic, presumably in metallic colors.

More typical are the mosaic, window, lighting, and woodwork by Tiffany Glass and Decorating Company that can be seen in the First Presbyterian Church in Bath, New York. Although the church building itself dates to earlier decades, in 1897 the interiors were completely redone by the Tiffany firm. The work included, in addition to its mosaics, a stone mosaic floor, sumptuous lighting fixtures, and a full complement of windows—all in a muted geometric, mosaic-like style. Byzantine mosaic patterning covers the three recessed surfaces of the niches in the chancel, as it does the pulpit and chancel rail.

After the Chicago world's fair Tiffany brought his exhibition chapel back to New York City where he placed it on display in his own showrooms, giving New Yorkers who were not able to make the trip to Chicago to see the chapel, another opportunity to do so even after the exposition had closed. This, no doubt, prompted city parishes in need of decoration to consider hiring Tiffany's ateliers, and several churches in New York City incorporated mosaic decoration into their interiors at the time of the World's Columbian Exposition and in subsequent years.

The church that perhaps above all others heralds the use of mosaics is St. Michael's and All Angels on the upper West Side of New York City.[32] It incorporates mosaics in different styles, and from two different periods, all by Tiffany. In Tiffany's initial work for the church, begun in 1895, he experimented with the close relationship between leaded-glass windows and mosaic work. In fact, some of his early windows were described in mosaic terms, and, like the windows at St. Hubert's, were intended to complement the use of mosaics. They were often, for example, in geometric designs and incorporated, in mosaic-like fashion, numerous small pieces of glass resembling tesserae. The treatment at the Church of St. Michael's and All Angels in New York is somewhat unusual. The apse of the church is divided into seven tall panels of angels with St. Michael in the central panel. The center five panels are extraordinarily tall and luminescent windows. The sixth and seventh panels, flanking each side, were described as mosaic panels. They received no outside light (today they are artificially lit from behind). Although the composition crosses over all seven panels, the challenge for Tiffany's studios was carrying this through with a change in medium as it reached the two end panels, which demanded reflected light rather than the traditional transmitted light of the windows. The resultant transition was subtle and effective.

Twenty-five years later, additional mosaics were added to the church and dedicated on Easter Sunday in 1920. The side chapel, or the Chapel of All Angels, was the focus of this renovation by Tiffany Studios, dominated by a large mosaic above the altar, and erected in memory of Margaret Elizabeth Zimmerman (fig. 43). The subject of the figural composition is angels amidst clouds and sky, the whole an extraordinary confection "in beautiful iridescent colors, pearl tints shading through gold to blue."[33] Mosaic pilasters frame the mosaic, and a pair of freestanding columns stand on either side of the altar. Relating to the columns of the Chicago chapel, the

---

[32] St. Michael's and All Angels Episcopal Church is located at Amsterdam Avenue and 99th Street, New York City. R. W. Gibson was the architect.

[33] "Glass Mosaic Masterpiece," *New York Times* (February 17, 1920), 8.

43. Mosaic above the altar, Chapel of All Angels, Church of St. Michael's and All Angels, 225 West 99th Street, New York City, completed 1920. Tiffany Studios. Photograph by Bruce Schwartz.

St. Michael's columns are completely encrusted with glass mosaic in slightly varying shades of iridescent blue. The shading starts at the very top with a lighter blue that descends gradually, all the while getting subtly darker and darker, to an almost midnight blue at the base. The blue is punctuated by small crosses in gold mosaic, the crosses themselves merging together to form a geometric decorative pattern. The columns, however, relate most closely to a pair of earlier columns made for the Tiffany Studios showroom. These were prominently displayed in front of a pair of portieres with a golden diapered fringe and tassels extending from the rod (fig. 44). The ornamentation of the columns replicates that on the portieres completely, illustrating Tiffany's extraordinary attention to detail (fig. 45).

Mosaics are an integral part of a much larger interior scheme by Tiffany Glass and Decorating Company at St. Paul's Church in Troy, New York, which was part of a remodeling the church undertook beginning in 1893. The extraordinary decorative ensemble—a rare survival—includes mosaics, wall stenciling, altar rail, windows, and lighting, all executed presumably under Holzer's direction. The chancel is richly ornamented. A tall dado on both sides is completely faced in gold mosaic, featuring gold foil-backed ribbed glass tesserae of two sizes arranged in a subtle patterning of crosses. The reredos features four square mosaic panels depicting the archangel Michael, the Virgin Mary, Jesus's disciple James, and archangel Gabriel. Recalling the Willard Memorial in Auburn of similar date, the floor is of cream, pink, and green marble and stone mosaic. Even the stenciled wall decoration recalls mosaic in its geometric patterning.

It was the ecclesiastical arm of the Tiffany firm that was responsible for the making of all wall mosaics. As it had inspired commissions in churches, the Tiffany Chapel exhibited at the Chicago world's fair of 1893 had a direct influence on the firm's obtaining commissions for important public buildings, like the Marquette Building and the Chicago Public Library, as we have seen. It also may have served as the impetus for domestic interior commissions, and it paved the way for more widespread use of mosaic in houses. One very personal commission for Tiffany must have been that of Emily Johnston and Robert W. de Forest. Robert de Forest was the brother of Lockwood de Forest, with whom Tiffany had partnered during the earliest years of his work in decoration. Tiffany was also related to the de Forest family through his second wife's family. The de Forests as newlyweds in the 1870s moved into her mother's Greek revival townhouse on Washington Square in New York. When they decided to expand in 1893-94, they invited their friend Tiffany to design a new addition of a library that would extend into the garden beyond.

A few invaluable black and white photographs give some idea of the inventiveness and virtuosity at

44. Pair of columns made for Tiffany Studios showroom, shown in showroom in front of portieres with fringe and tassels, ca. 1905. Historic photograph, Morse Museum of American Art (2000-024:004).

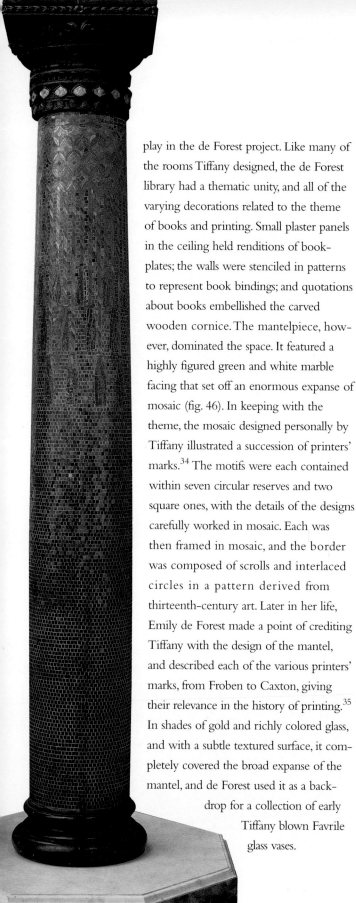

play in the de Forest project. Like many of the rooms Tiffany designed, the de Forest library had a thematic unity, and all of the varying decorations related to the theme of books and printing. Small plaster panels in the ceiling held renditions of book-plates; the walls were stenciled in patterns to represent book bindings; and quotations about books embellished the carved wooden cornice. The mantelpiece, how-ever, dominated the space. It featured a highly figured green and white marble facing that set off an enormous expanse of mosaic (fig. 46). In keeping with the theme, the mosaic designed personally by Tiffany illustrated a succession of printers' marks.[34] The motifs were each contained within seven circular reserves and two square ones, with the details of the designs carefully worked in mosaic. Each was then framed in mosaic, and the border was composed of scrolls and interlaced circles in a pattern derived from thirteenth-century art. Later in her life, Emily de Forest made a point of crediting Tiffany with the design of the mantel, and described each of the various printers' marks, from Froben to Caxton, giving their relevance in the history of printing.[35] In shades of gold and richly colored glass, and with a subtle textured surface, it com-pletely covered the broad expanse of the mantel, and de Forest used it as a back-drop for a collection of early Tiffany blown Favrile glass vases.

46. Above: Fireplace wall with mosaic decoration by Louis Comfort Tiffany for the library of Emily Johnston and Robert W. de Forest house, 7 Washington Square, New York, ca. 1895-1900. Photograph courtesy of Priscilla de Forest Williams.

45. Left: Mosaic column made for Tiffany Studios showroom, ca. 1905. From studio building at Laurelton Hall, Cold Spring Harbor, Long Island, New York. Favrile glass, cement, plaster capital, 11 ft. 1 in. (339 cm). The Metropolitan Museum of Art, Purchase, The Edgar J. Kaufmann Charitable Foundation Gift, 1968. (68.184).

Perhaps Tiffany's most lavish and unusual use of mosaic decoration in a domestic context occurred in the house he designed in 1899 at 395 Common-wealth Avenue in Boston, Massachusetts. The house is further testament of Tiffany's love of Islamic art, and its interpretation in the medium that he made his own. As he had in the Vanderbilt and Havemeyer houses, for example, Tiffany pushed the medium yet again, and created something completely different, at once theatrical and refined. It is not known what prompted Mr. and Mrs. Frederick Ayer, in conserva-tive Boston, to decide to make the daring selection of Louis Tiffany to design their new home. The couple traveled widely, making an extended trip to Turkey and Egypt just prior to the building of their house, and their taste for Near Eastern art and architecture meshed perfectly with Tiffany's. They had earlier trav-eled to Chicago in 1893 to see the World's

---

34 Emily Johnston de Forest, "The House, 7 Washington Square and an Inventory of its contents," typescript, April 1928, [p. 27]. The Metropolitan Museum of Art, Department of Drawings and Prints (1971.645).

35 Ibid.

Columbian Exposition, and undoubtedly were among those visitors to Tiffany's impressive display there, where in his extraordinary chapel his mosaic work was so compellingly shown to the public. Indeed, Tiffany adapted several features of that exhibition chapel to his designs for the Ayer house. When Frederick Ayer and his young wife, Ellen, approached Tiffany to design their house, as he had for the Havemeyers seven years earlier, the designer found a perfect artist-patron relationship. One senses that Tiffany was given tremendous freedom to experiment, to try something altogether new in this extraordinary house.

Little is known about the architect of record of the house, A. J. Manning, giving rise to the speculation that Tiffany himself was more involved with the architecture, inside and out, on this building than was typically the case. Manning had previously worked with Tiffany on a project in Tarrytown, New York, where the Tiffany family had a country place.[36] The Ayer house is most unusual in its interpretation of Near Eastern designs and its homage to mosaic, which Tiffany even incorporated on the exterior of the building. Stone and glass mosaic ornament decorates the cornice and corbels, square panels between the upper-story windows, and the framework surrounding the entrance (fig. 47). It was a completely novel idea to announce the thematic ornament of the interior design on the exterior façade. Here, the Islamic-inspired mosaic panels that flank the front door, in stone and glass in shades of red, orange, and gold, correspond in both design and palette to the mosaic-like transom windows in the drawing room (fig. 48). It is as

47. Stone and glass mosaic ornament by Louis Comfort Tiffany on the exterior cornice and corbels of the Frederick and Ellen Ayer House, 395 Commonwealth Avenue, Boston, 1899. Photograph by Richard Cheek.

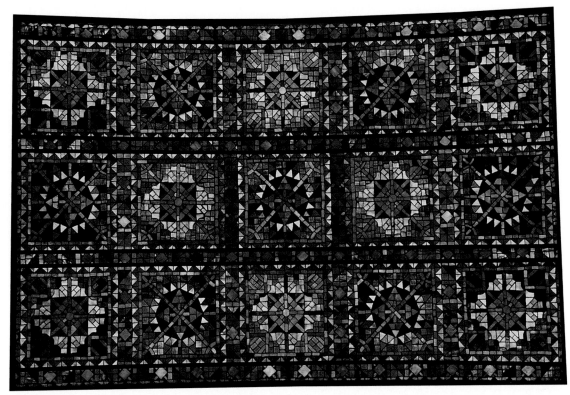

48. Transom window by Louis Comfort Tiffany in the drawing room of the Ayer House. Photograph by Richard Cheek.

if the exterior panel has been turned ninety degrees, and repeated three times to make up just one of three of the transom windows, which when seen under reflected light give the appearance of a mosaic itself. In a similar relationship, the lunette over the door is echoed in the decoration of the mantelpiece, similar in its palette of blue, green, and gold, as well as its use of the six-pointed Islamic star in the design (fig. 49).

The avant-garde façade merely hints at the unusual entrance hall and staircase. The floor is composed of thousands of marble tesserae in subtle chalky tones, and the nearly six-and-one-half-foot-high white marble dado is delineated by a narrow decorative geometric border of green and blue

mosaic. Overhead, originally suspended from a stained-glass skylight on the fifth floor, hangs a globe fixture aptly described in a 1903 inventory of the house, as "of mosaic in clouded and corrugated glass" that is en suite with the cool marble and mosaic tones of the room (fig. 50).[37] Additional lighting is provided from the glow through three Favrile-glass blown globes, miraculous survivals, which still remain in their mosaic glass niches.

A series of steps with rounded profiles lead up to a stage-like landing before further ascending to the

[36] Helen Gould, an important patron of Tiffany's may have been responsible for bringing Tiffany and Manning together. Tiffany and Manning collaborated on a reading room in the Irvington Public Library in the Irvington Town Hall of 1901-1902. Tiffany's involvement in the project was stipulated by Miss Gould, who contributed the money for the interior decorations of the room. Here, too, mosaic was used extensively, in a palette of rich peacock blue, as full-height door and window surrounds. Alfred J. Manning lived in Irvington, and his architectural offices were located at 121 East 23rd Street, just around the corner from Tiffany's. In addition to the Ayer house, Tiffany and Manning were both involved in "Rochroane," the forty-four room castle in Irvington-on-Hudson built for oil and cotton baron Melchior S. Belthoover completed in 1905. That house featured enormous Gothic paneling and a large landscape window, with hollyhocks, trumpet vine, and clematis, now in the Corning Museum of Glass. Nomination Form for National Register of Historic Places Inventory, for Irvington Village Hall, July 19, 1984. I am grateful to Barbara Denyer for sharing this information with me.

49. Decoration by Louis Comfort Tiffany over door in the Ayer House. Photograph by Richard Cheek.

landing from which the stairway splits and turns to the second floor. The steps themselves pay homage to the Chicago world's fair chapel, made of marble with risers decorated in green, blue, and gold glass mosaic. The ceiling is an expanse of shimmering gold glass mosaic of Byzantine splendor. Beyond the unusually theatrical architectural proscenium arch, and at the top of the stair landing, Tiffany created an exceedingly convincing trompe l'oeil mosaic of a Greek temple, complete with dome and columns (fig. 51). The effect is one of extraordinary depth, accentuated by an ingenious system of reflective mirrors and lights.

If the use of such shimmering and sumptuous mosaics conjured up images of luxury and the exotic past for a private individual, this evocation of grandeur was in turn deemed appropriate when applied to the

50. Entrance hall and staircase by Louis Comfort Tiffany in the Ayer House. Photograph by Richard Cheek.

[37] "Inventory of Household Effects of Residence of Frederick Ayer Esq.," typescript., 1903, n.p. [p.1]. Courtesy of Scott Steward.

51. Trompe l'oeil mosaic of a Greek temple by Louis Comfort Tiffany in the Ayer House. Photograph by Richard Cheek.

country's public buildings, like churches, museums, libraries, universities, and even to more commercial establishments such as banks or the newly built department store. Mosaic was the perfect medium to make this transition. It gave an immediate aesthetic gratification, bringing to mind visions of the splendors of Constantinople, and its qualities of durability and ease of cleansing added to its suitability for public spaces.

Just as mosaic was deemed appropriate embellishment for houses of worship, it was also highly suitable for houses of learning, whether a great library, as in the Chicago Public Library, discussed earlier, or in a grand auditorium, like Alexander Hall at Princeton University. The lack of recognition that this impressive, though slightly altered, interior has received is little indication of the importance attached to it by Tiffany in its own time. When the building was conceived as early as 1890, "as a worthy tribute to Learning," the architect William Potter was selected to design the imposing Romanesque Revival building. Louis C. Tiffany, with Jacob A. Holzer as the supervising artist, was chosen to decorate much of the interior.

Potter's relationship with Tiffany was further enhanced when Tiffany provided the decorations for

Potter's St. Agnes Church in New York City, completed in 1893 (no longer standing). The nave and chancel feature elaborate marble and mosaic decorations that relate closely to the Chicago exposition chapel. The lectern, Bishop's chair, altar, sedilia, altar rail, and pulpit are all of white marble inset with mosaic work of colored glass and stones. The decorations also include an enormous baptismal font (fig. 52).

In Princeton's Alexander Hall, the various sections of this complex architectural structure are united by their mosaic treatments. Inside each main vestibule of the building is a mosaic floor inlaid in

52. Period view of decorations from St. Agnes' Church, New York, 1893, illustrated in Tiffany Glass and Decorating Company, *Tiffany Glass Mosaics* (New York, 1896), opp. p. 5. The Metropolitan Museum of Art, Thomas J. Watson Library.

cosmatesque fashion with a design of five tangential circles. This same design is repeated again in some of the interior architectural elements. The facing of the rostrum, its two short flights of stairs, and side and near walls are composed of Tiffany's blue, green, white, and gold glass inset into highly figured Sienna marble. The focal point, however, is a large mosaic frieze made in three panels, displayed high on the wall at the rear of the rostrum and facing the assembly (fig. 53). The imposing panels of figures in classical garb arranged in a frieze-like fashion reveal a highly thought-out and appropriate iconography depicting the Homeric story. At the center is "The Song of Homer," with Homer portrayed seated amidst the heroes and heroines he wrote about in the The Illiad and The Odyssey. The flanking panels display figures readying for the Trojan War: the Greeks with weapons in hand on one side, and the Trojan warriors with chariot and horses on the other (fig. 54).[38] Holzer yet again was responsible for the mosaics, and admirably reveals his affinity for the medium. Particularly noteworthy are the subtle shadings of the robes and figures in the innumerable cut tesserae of Favrile glass.

Tiffany continued to exhibit his work at international exhibitions: at the Grafton Galleries in London, for example, in 1899; at the Paris exposition of 1900; and at Turin in 1902. At the London venue in 1899, in addition to the numerous and heralded examples of his Favrile glass vases, enamels, lamps, and windows, Tiffany exhibited a number of samples, or prototypes, of his firm's mosaics. These included a

large mosaic altar-piece of *The Last Supper*, from designs by figural window designer Frederick Wilson (1858-1932). *The Last Supper* was later installed in a church in Baltimore. Tiffany's studios kept a full-size prototype of St. Andrew from that mosaic mural, which remained in the studios until it closed.[39] In addition, Tiffany exhibited a sample from the frieze at the Marquette Building, of a North American Indian, part of the frieze of the Delivery Room in the Chicago Public Library, plus some more domestic items, like a mantelpiece and a mirror frame.[40] Many of these were also exhibited at the Paris fair of 1900.

In addition to mosaics, Tiffany exhibited to great acclaim a spectacular *Resurrection* window at the Paris exposition. Again, the international critical exposure and acclaim that Tiffany received at the exhibition was important for generating new business. The family of Jeptha Homer Wade, founder of Western Union Telegraph in Cleveland, had seen the *Resurrection* window that Tiffany had exhibited there and commissioned him to make that the focal point of an entire decorative scheme for a grand chapel in memory of their loved one. The Wade Memorial Chapel in Lake View Cemetery in

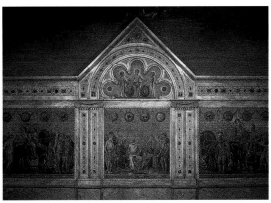

53. Mosaic frieze by Jacob Holzer for Tiffany Studios in Alexander Commencement Hall, Princeton University, Princeton, New Jersey, ca. 1890. Photograph Princeton University.

[38] For an extensive description of Alexander Hall, see Greta M. Rubinow, "An In-Depth Study of Alexander Hall," Senior Thesis (Princeton University), typescript, 1973.

[39] This panel is currently at Lillian Nassau, Ltd., New York City.

[40] Grafton Galleries, *Exhibition of L'Art Nouveau, S. Bing, Paris* (London: Grafton Galleries), exhibition catalogue, (1899).

54. Mosaic frieze panel detail of Trojan warriors, Alexander Commencement Hall.

Cleveland, Ohio (1899-1900) features two large mosaic panels extending the full length of the chapel on either side, each about twenty-five feet in length (fig. 55). As was typical, the floor is of stone mosaic, and the architectural details, including the ceiling, are of white marble. Like the mosaics in the Marquette Building in Chicago and Alexander Hall at Princeton, the subject of these panels is narrative in tone. The mosaics that run down each side of the mausoleum feature complementary compositions of, on one side, a barge with seven Old Testament prophets and seven rowers, and on the other, a barge with seven figures from the New Testament and seven rowers. Frederick Wilson, an Englishman who was one of the primary designers of Tiffany figural windows and who also designed mosaics, prepared the ingenious composition of the frieze-like figures and allegorical oarsmen. The

durability of mosaics may have dictated their choice as a decorative medium, for Mr. Wade's son and primary instigator for the chapel said, "I want to make sure it will last for at least five hundred years."[41]

In 1902-1905 when Tiffany worked on his dream house, the country estate that he built for himself in Oyster Bay, Long Island, overlooking Long Island Sound, he incorporated many of the decorative treatments that he had utilized during his career up to that date, including mosaics. In this exotic and fanciful building, mosaic decoration played a subordinate role to the collections that inhabited it. They were most notable in the floor of the Fountain Court, the aesthetic center of the house (fig. 56). Decorative patterning, reminiscent of an Islamic mosque was divided into rectangular panels surrounding the central octagonal fountain. The fountain itself featured mosaic decoration with its irregular blue iridescent tesserae lining the bottom of the pool and enhancing the shimmering

[41] Quoted in Michael Curtis, "Glory in Glass," *The Magazine of Case Western Reserve University* (November 1991), n.p.

55. Mosaic panel by Frederick Wilson for Tiffany Studios in Wade Memorial Chapel, Lake View Cemetery, Cleveland, Ohio, 1899-1900. Photograph Lake View Cemetery.

effect of the water. One wall of the first-floor dining room—seemingly modernist in feeling and architecture—featured mosaic decoration inlaid onto the marble chimney breast in shades of blue and green that recalls the decorated mantel in the Ayer house (fig. 57). At Laurelton the Islamic motifs were replaced by three mosaic glass dials, which were illuminated at night, one to mark the time of the day, one for the day of the week, and one for the date.

In Chicago in 1907, in proximity to the Chicago Public Library, retail merchant Marshall Field built his famed eponymous department store, designed by the firm of Daniel Burnham and Company. The scheme called for an immense dome spanning the fifth and sixth floors. Executed by Tiffany Studios, it gives the impression of a shimmering starlit blue sky, covering an area of six thousand square feet. It incorporates more than one and one-half million pieces of iridescent Favrile glass, predominantly of various colors of blue, displayed in a wave-like design. Before the store opened to the public in September of 1907, it was said that fifty craftsmen worked for two years to complete the mosaic.[42] The scale of the Marshall Field & Company mosaic dome paved the way for the firm's subsequent work.

Within a five-year period from 1910 to 1915, Tiffany Studios undertook three monumental

56. Interior view of Laurelton Hall entrance hall with fountain. Photograph ca. 1920, by David Aranow. The Metropolitan Museum of Art, Gift of Robert Koch, 1978. (1978.646.18).

works in mosaic, a mosaic curtain for the National Theatre in the City of Mexico, completed in 1911, the Roman Catholic Cathedral in St. Louis, Missouri, completed in 1912, and the *Dream Garden*, the spectacular mosaic mural after a Maxfield Parrish painting commissioned by the Curtis Publishing Company for its headquarters in Philadelphia, completed in 1915. All three commissions represent a tour de force of the use of mosaic, and are a testament to the extraordinary skill of the mosaic workers in the Tiffany Studios employ. At the same time, they represent a departure from Tiffany Studios' execution of designs prepared by in-house designers; in these examples, the studios executed mosaics of the designs of artists who were selected specially for the various commissions.

In 1911 the City of Mexico built a large theater as part of a grander project to build a num-

57. Fireplace wall at Laurelton Hall in the collection of Morse Museum of American Art, featuring mosaic decoration inlaid onto marble chimney breast. Photo in Samuel Howe, "An American Country House," *International Studio*, vol. 33, no.132 (February 1908), 296. Courtesy Metropolitan Museum of Art, Watson Library.

ber of public buildings designed to adorn the city. The theater itself is a rich compendium of styles and materials, set in a lush garden interspersed with fountains and pergolas. The resulting building is massive in size, designed by the Mexican architect Adamo Boari. Inside, its curtain of glass mosaic received particular attention. The medium was initially chosen for its fire-resistant properties, and experiments were initiated with Bohemian and Venetian glass. The original design was credited to a Mexican artist, Dr. Atl, who created the program for a modello painted by Harry Stoner, a painter and stage designer retained by Tiffany.[43] The natural beauties of Mexico inspired the grand design, which is a dramatic landscape scene of the snow-capped peaks of Ixtaccihuatl and Popocatepetl above luxuriant valleys (fig. 58).

In addition to exploring the pictorial possibilities of such a scene in glass, the mosaic curtain was considered a technical marvel. It was said to be supported by a steel frame, and the entire construction to weigh twenty-one tons. It was to be raised and lowered by a special hydraulic elevating device operated by two motors. The mosaic itself was said to contain over a million tesserae of Tiffany's Favrile glass.[44] The mosaic was shipped to Mexico City in 1911, after it had been put on exhibition for one month in the Tiffany Studios in April of that year.[45] According to Leslie Nash, the foreman of the Tiffany Studios at the time of the mosaic's execution, the making of the glass took almost three years. Nash also claimed that the iridescent glass mosaic was intended to ornament the exterior

[42] Sharon Darling, , *Chicago Ceramics & Glass* (Chicago: Chicago Historical Society, 1979), 137.

[43] Robert Koch, *Louis C. Tiffany: Rebel in Glass* (New York: Crown Publiishers, Inc., 1966 (reissued ed.), 84, 116.

58. City of Mexico National Theatre mosaic curtain containing over a million tesserae of Tiffany's Favrile glass. Historic photo courtesy Metropolitan Museum of Art.

dome "so that it could have been seen for miles but the cost was so high that it was abandoned."[46]

The Mexico City curtain may have been the inspiration for the Curtis Publishing Company's *Dream Garden* mosaic at its headquarters in Philadelphia. Tiffany may first have produced a smaller luminescent garden landscape mosaic and fountain to submit on speculation to the Curtis Publishing Company for installation in its Philadelphia headquarters.[47] Currently installed in the Charles Engelhard Court of The American Wing Court of The Metropolitan Museum of Art, it features tall cypress trees in the background with a placid pool of water marked only by the narrow ripple carved by two swans gently gliding on the pond (fig. 59). A wall, plinth, and urn of stone in the classic taste provide a compositional anchor and foil for the bounteous flowers, including the urn, literally bursting with pink and red roses, an amusing contrast with the simple terra cotta flower pot resting on the plinth and potted with a single red rose. The sky contrasts with the rest of the panel in its subtle, iridescent blues, greens, and pinks. However beautiful, the garden landscape was rejected by the Philadelphia company, and the mosaic and land-

scape graced the Tiffany Studios showrooms as evidence of the firm's work until those rooms closed down in 1934.

The Curtis Publishing Company instead settled on a collaboration between Louis Tiffany and the Philadelphia artist and illustrator Maxfield Parrish. The pairing was the brainchild of Edward Bok, editor of *Ladies Home Journal*, the signature magazine for the Curtis Publishing Company. Tiffany's luminous opalescent and iridescent glass was a perfect medium with which to depict Parrish's designs. The result, completed in 1915, was a monumental mosaic, fifteen feet high and forty-nine feet long set in a specially designed marble-faced platform and frame in the entrance hall of the company's headquarters on Independence Square. This was the largest mosaic project Tiffany had ever undertaken. Maxfield

59. Louis Comfort Tiffany. Tiffany Studios. Mosaic wall mural of garden landscape and fountain, ca. 1905-15. Favrile glass, cement. Mosaic: 8 ft. 7 in. (262.9 cm); Fountain and base: 24 in. (61 cm). The Metropolitan Museum of Art, Gift of Lillian Nassau, 1976, and Gift of Mrs. L. Groves Geer, 1978. (1976.105, 1978.584).

[44] See Martin Eidelberg and Nancy McClelland, *Behind the Scenes of Tiffany Glassmaking: The Nash Notebooks* (New York: St. Martin's Press, in association with Christie's Fine Art Auctioneers), 2001, 101-102.

[45] Tiffany Studios, *Mosaic Curtain for the National Theatre of Mexico* (New York: Tiffany Studios, 1911), n.p.. Collection of The Metropolitan Museum of Art.

[46] Eidelberg and McClelland, 102.

[47] Hand-written marginal notes by Leslie H. Nash in his personal copy of *Tiffany Studios, Memorials in Glass and Stone* (New York: Tiffany Studios Ecclesiastical Department, 1913). Christie's, New York, Estate of Leslie H. Nash. Sale (December 8, 2000).

60. Design by Maxfield Parrish. Tiffany Studios. *Dream Garden*, completed 1915. Favrile glass mosaic, 15 x 49 ft. Located in Curtis Publishing Company headquarters, Philadelphia. Photograph by Jeffrey Totaro.

Parrish's art, with its golden light-filled idyllic landscapes, was ideally suited to be interpreted in Tiffany's lustrous Favrile glass (fig. 60). The mosaic snow-capped mountains are seen in illusionistic fashion with rocky boulders and lush foliage in the foreground. According to a small pamphlet published by the Curtis Publishing Company about the installation, it had taken Parrish many months to produce the original painting.[48] Then, the painting's infinite mysteries had to be interpreted in a new medium, which Tiffany had begun at that time to take to even greater heights. Tiffany's glass afforded a tremendous variety—lustrous, transparent, opaque, and opalescent, each with its own texture, and in an infinite range of colors. He altered the traditional shape and size of glass tesserae, vary-ing it widely throughout one composition to bet-ter convey the desired motifs. As was said in the pamphlet, "Never before has it been possible to give the perspective in mosaics as it is shown in this picture, and the most remarkable and beautiful effect is secured when different lights play upon this completed mosaic."[49] The author continued on to say that "the mountains recede, the trees and foliage stand out distinctly, and as the light changes, the purple shadows will creep slowly from the base of the mountain to its top; that the canions [sic] and the waterfalls, the thickets and the flowers, all tell their story and interpret Mr. Parrish's dream."[50]

For more than two thousand years the tech-nique of mosaics changed little. Mosaic work was fabricated in the late nineteenth century in essen-tially the same method as by the earliest workers in the medium. It required the skills of the mosaic

[48] *The Dream Garden* (Philadelphia, Pennsylvania: The Curtis Publishing Company, n.d.).

craftsman, or musivarius, and the artist, or mosaicist. The musivarius was first and foremost an individual possessed of dexterity and skill, and he or she also had to have color sense and aesthetic intuition as well. Tiffany felt that women were the most talented in the field because of their high degree of handi-work. He employed numbers of women who had been trained at one of several art schools in New York City (fig. 61). In 1898 about twenty women were employed in the mosaic shop. With no work-ing experience, women—hired out of the Art Students League, Cooper Institute School of Applied Design, and the art department of the YWCA—started out as apprentices with Tiffany. He felt that members of the female sex were espe-cially desirable for mosaic work because it required great patience, and "their manual dexterity to cut tesserae and keen color sense" was particularly well suited for the work. Their desirability not with-standing, problems were also cited: "...young girls constantly getting married and nearly disrupts the workshop."[51] This is born out by the fact that most of the women in his employ were not married.

In 1898 Clara Wolcott Driscoll (1881-1945), who already had worked as a designer for the firm, was put in charge of the mosaic department. Tiffany had confidence in Driscoll, with whom he traveled to Europe, together with fellow window designer Agnes Northrop (1857-1953), and scientist Dr. McIllhenny in the summer of 1907. Among the few workers in mosaics who have been identified, in addition to Driscoll, are Minnie Henderson and Marian Palmie, who were reported to have worked

on a mosaic panel for a church in Boston in 1899.

The sequence of steps involved from the original commission to completion was similar to the execution of a stained-glass window. First, a small-scale watercolor sketch was prepared to work out the composition and color scheme, often with the suggestion of individual tesserae (fig. 62). Following that, the studios might craft a small maquette of a section of the mosaic which would suggest to the client the arrangement of colors and materials. One rare surviving example, perhaps origi-nally for a church interior, features individual tesserae

61. Interior view of mosaic shop with woman craftsman at work. Illustrated in Tiffany Glass and Decorating Company *Tiffany Glass Mosaics* (New York 1896), following p. 16. The Metropolitan Museum of Art, Thomas J. Watson Library.

49 Ibid.

50 Ibid.

51 *New York Daily Tribune*, January 16, 1898.

of Favrile glass, mother-of-pearl, and opal affixed to a wooden panel that would suggest the embellishment for a decorative architectural treatment (fig. 63).[52] Subsequently, the mosaicists would begin their work, often producing a full-scale section of the final commission. In an interior view of the Mosaic Department at the Tiffany Studios building in New York (fig. 64), one can see an array of partial mosaics or maquettes displayed on the shelves and walls of the workroom. Some of these full-scale mosaic details, such as the numerous square panels, each distinguished by a different geometric pattern, may also have served as suggested decorative treatments for future commissions. It is interesting to note that the mosaic workroom that was included as one of the important areas of production for the studios, depicts in reality few artisans working directly on mosaics. It seems that the workroom was shared by men fabricating leaded-glass lampshades that can be seen on many of the worktables in the room.

Historically, the traditional method of composing a mosaic involved individual pieces of glass that were cut into the squares of uniform size and shape, and the effects of light and shade, perspective and other details of design were given scant consideration. Tiffany, as he had done earlier in windows, desired to produce a more faithful illusionistic design in mosaic, and yet this was not possible with the historic application of the medium, which utilized glass in solid, even colors. Therefore, as he had achieved color variations within a single piece of glass for his windows, so too was he able to achieve a similar effect in mosaic. The traditional square tesserae, each of similar size and shape, were replaced in Tiffany's examples by a freer interpretation. The individual pieces were cut in varied shapes to conform more faithfully to the rendered design. This helped to enhance compositional details. Tiffany also made some innovations in the cement or bonding agent he used, an important ingredient in the making of mosaics. He claimed to employ something called Keene's cement, "or in a hydraulic or oleaginous cement where it is exposed to the weather and moisture."[53]

He did not make his mosaics on site as did the ancients. Nor did he employ the so-called later, or indirect method where mosaic work was composed face-down upon paper or cast in slabs before it was affixed to the wall. Tiffany's mosaics were always worked face to, so that the craftsman could see every detail and so the artist could not only see the evolving work, but could "direct the whole operation, correcting mistakes and making alterations with the same ease as a painter in oil."[54]

The color field of Tiffany's mosaic glass was far broader than previously known and was capable of retaining gradations of tone and shadings in one piece, also hitherto unknown. Whereby historic mosaics, although rich in effect, were practically devoid of

62. Facing page, bottom: Louis Comfort Tiffany. Tiffany Glass and Decorating Company or Tiffany Studios. Drawing for lunette of cornucopia, ca. 1900-1910, watercolor, graphite, brown ink, and gouache; rice-paper border attached to drawing, 11 3/8 x 17 in. (28.9 x 44.5 cm). The Metropolitan Museum of Art, Purchase, Walter Hoving and Julia T. Weld Gifts and Dodge Fund, 1967. (67.654.466).

63. Left: Design by Louis Comfort Tiffany, Tiffany Studios. Maquette for interior mosaic decoration, ca. 1895-1905. Wood, Favrile glass, mother-of-pearl, leather, and opal, 8 5/8 x 6 in. (21.9 x 15.2 cm). This maquette was owned by Joseph Briggs, manager of the Tiffany Studios through the 1920s. The Metropolitan Museum of Art, Gift of Mr. And Mrs. Samuel Schwartz, 1984. (1984.179).

64. Below: Interior view of Mosaics Shop, illustrated in Tiffany Studios *Character and Individuality in Decorations and Furnishings* (New York: Tiffany Studios, 1913), n.p. The Metropolitan Museum of Art, Thomas J. Watson Library.

shading and modeling, in Tiffany's mosaics, with its limitless range of color and color gradations, every detail of a composition could be faithfully replicated.

New decorative possibilities opened up with the use of Tiffany's distinctive luster or iridescent glass, whereby the luminosity of a twilight sky or the brilliancy of a peacock's plumage, or the shimmer of the oily surface of fish scales could be given full expression. The result was no longer flat, but uncannily illusionistic, without sacrificing the richness of color and material. In so doing, Tiffany was able to inject his mosaic compositions with a subtlety, inviting the viewer to linger and absorb all the details that would become apparent only after longer study.

[52] This maquette has a provenance from the estate of Joseph Briggs, former superintendent of the Tiffany Studios.

[53] Tiffany Glass & Decorating Company, *Glass Mosaic* (New York, 1896), 18.

[54] Ibid.

Tiffany Glass and Decorating Company at The World's Columbian Exposition

by Joel M. Hoffman

At the 1893 World's Columbian Exposition in Chicago, the Tiffany Glass and Decorating Company exhibited the chapel now installed at the Morse Museum, various other ecclesiastical furnishings, and two decorated rooms.[1] Louis Comfort Tiffany's chroniclers have repeatedly referred to the Chicago world's fair as a watershed in the designer's career. Hugh McKean, for example, in The "Lost" Treasures of Louis Comfort Tiffany, *wrote that the exhibit earned Tiffany a position of artistic leadership in America and launched his career in Europe.[2] Likewise, Alastair Duncan, in the second sentence of his "Introduction" to* Masterworks of Louis Comfort Tiffany, *declared 1893 as "the time Tiffany rose to public eminence."[3] And Robert Koch, in* Louis C. Tiffany: Rebel in Glass, *characterized the chapel as "the apex of Tiffany's Neo-Byzantine ecclesiastical interiors."[4]*

Promotional materials produced both by Tiffany and by the World's Columbian Exposition, together with contemporary accounts of the 1893 fair, are helpful in looking at the objectives and impact of Tiffany Glass and Decorating Company exhibits at the Chicago fair from another viewpoint. These documents demonstrate that Tiffany astutely used the World's Columbian Exposition to promote his firm as the preeminent provider of stained glass, ecclesiastical furnishings, and residential interiors for affluent clients in the United States and Europe. While the fair had a major impact upon Louis Comfort Tiffany's burgeoning business, the impact occurred in ways not yet fully described.

The era of international expositions opened with London's Great Exhibition of 1851, which was housed in Joseph Paxton's prefabricated iron-and-glass Crystal Palace (fig. 65). Like the international expositions that succeeded it, the Great Exhibition was intended to showcase the arts and industry of the time, particularly those of the host country, and to foster peaceful partnership and trade among participant nations. The nineteenth-century world's fairs afforded millions of visitors access to new technological and artistic products, thereby spurring comparison, competition, and consumption. Many of the world's fairs had a proprietary theme, commemorating an historic event. All bore a host of political, economic, social, and cultural subtexts, often aimed at consolidating or enhancing individual, group, or national power. The Great Exhibition of 1851, for example, encouraged the development of British industry, played a formative role in the creation of what is now the Victoria and Albert Museum, and vindicated Queen Victoria's unpopular royal consort, Prince Albert, one of the exhibition's principal supporters.[5] World's fairs also offered new forms of entertainment, some of which revolved around ethnology exhibits and vicarious travel to foreign lands.[6]

---

[1] The author acknowledges Patricia Pongracz Spicka for her research of 1996, now published as a chapter, "The Chapel's First Installation and Move to Saint John the Divine," in this book. Spicka's account was critical in apprising the author of several important primary documents used herein.

[2] Hugh McKean, *The "Lost" Treasures of Louis Comfort Tiffany* (Garden City: Doubleday and Company, Inc., 1980; reissue Atglen, PA: Shiffer Publishing, 2002), 137-38.

[3] Alastair Duncan, "Introduction," in *Masterworks of Louis Comfort Tiffany* (New York: Harry N. Abrams, Inc., 1989), 7.

[4] Robert Koch, *Louis C. Tiffany: Rebel in Glass* (New York: Crown Publishers, Inc., 1982), 76.

[5] Reid Badger, *The Great American Fair: The World's Columbian Exposition and American Culture* (Chicago: Nelson Hall, 1979), 3-6.

[6] Robert W. Rydell, *All the World's a Fair* (Chicago: The University of Chicago Press, 1984), 2.

Between 1851 and 1900 nearly one hundred international expositions were held.[7] Some of these fairs are all but forgotten, while others have been recognized as major cultural events. Subsequent to the Great Exhibition, world's fairs increasingly addressed natural history, science, agriculture, education, and the fine arts. The larger fairs took place primarily in Western Europe and the United States, though some were mounted in less-developed countries. It was commonly asserted, as a point of pride, that the greatest exhibit of a world's fair was the city in which it was held, for major international expositions could only take place in major metropolitan centers. Among the great host cities, Paris, in particular, mounted a series of five Expositions Universelles between 1855 and 1900.[8] The first major American world's fair was the Philadelphia Centennial International Exhibition of 1876, commemorating the hundredth anniversary of the Declaration of Independence. Technology was the highlight of the Centennial Exhibition, which included such innovations as the telephone, the typewriter, the sewing machine, and the massive Corliss steam engine. American exhibits of fine and industrial arts at the Philadelphia fair were considered lackluster. The Centennial Exhibition did, however, provide important visibility for the decorative arts of other nations, most notably Japan and France. Art glass gained particular

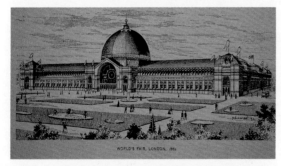

65. The Crystal Palace. From Hubert Howe Bancroft, *The Book of the Fair* (Chicago and San Francisco: The Bancroft Company, Publishers, 1893). The Mitchell Wolfson Jr. Collection, The Wolfsonian-Florida International University, Miami Beach, Florida.

prominence, and following the 1876 exposition there emerged in America an increased demand for decorative arts in what became known as the "Artistic Craze."[9] Before decisively embracing the decorative arts, Louis Comfort Tiffany exhibited his oil paintings and watercolors at world's fairs in Philadelphia and Paris.[10]

The 1893 World's Columbian Exposition surpassed the Philadelphia world's fair as the most elaborate and extensive public exhibition mounted in the United States in the nineteenth century (figs. 66, 67). Organizers boasted that the Chicago fair significantly overshadowed its predecessors, specifically in Paris and Philadelphia, relative to overall acreage, building area, number of buildings, cost of buildings, and area of exhibition space.[11] The World's Columbian Exposition commemorated the four-hundredth anniversary of Christopher Columbus's landing in America—but even official publications acknowledged that this was merely a pretext for the fair, its "sentimental side."[12] In fact the project was founded on ambitious objectives surrounding the advancement of American commerce and culture. The World's Columbian Exposition showcased American progress and prosperity, though it was mounted during widespread industrial depression.[13] Historian Robert Rydell explains that, by promoting America's wares, the 1893 fair was designed to facilitate this country's economic penetration into foreign markets as a means of ameliorating the negative

7 Robert W. Rydell, "Rediscovering the 1893 Chicago World's Columbian Exposition," in *Revisiting the White City: American Art at the 1893 World's Fair* (Hanover: University Press of New England, 1993), 20.

8 Badger, *The Great American Fair*, 8, 10.

9 Badger, *The Great American Fair*, 17; and Alice Cooney Frelinghuysen, *Louis Comfort Tiffany at The Metropolitan Museum* (New York: *The Metropolitan Museum of Art Bulletin* 56, Summer 1998), 53.

10 Koch, 8-9.

impact of domestic overproduction.[14] Among the fair's impressive American products, highlighted in John J. Flinn's 1893 *The Best Things to Be Seen at the World's Fair*, were the illumination of buildings and grounds by electric light, the electric boat launch and railway, and a host of powerful engines.[15] Equally impressive was the 260-foot-tall Ferris Wheel on the mile-long Midway Plaisance, where exhibits on non-Western cultures met other forms of popular entertainment, including balloon rides, Algerian bellydancers, and animal shows.[16]

As a Beaux Arts wonderland, the World's Columbian Exposition also promoted American architecture and fine arts. Dubbed the "White City," the Chicago world's fair was composed of exhibit palaces by America's most renowned Classicists, including Richard Morris Hunt, George B. Post, and McKim, Mead and White. Consulting architects Daniel H. Burnham and John W. Root had recommended the architects and the style. Conceived as a unified work of art, the World's Columbian Exposition was also distinguished by its program of decorative sculpture, orchestrated by Augustus St. Gaudens. John J. Flinn observed of the fair: "In the fall of 1892, there were collected in Chicago probably the greatest corps of American artists ever brought

66. The World's Columbian Exposition, looking southwest from the roof of the Manufactures and Liberal Arts Building at (from left to right) the Agricultural Building, Machinery Hall, and Administration Building. From James W. Shepp and Daniel B. Shepp, *Shepp's World's Fair Photographed* (Chicago: Globe Bible Publishing Co., 1893). The Mitchell Wolfson Jr. Collection, The Wolfsonian-Florida International University.

67. Frederick MacMonnie's *Columbian Fountain* in the Court of Honor (foreground); also (from left to right in background) Agricultural Building, The Colonnade, and Machinery Hall. From J.W. Buel, *The Magic City: A Massive Portfolio of Original Photographic Views of the Great World's Fair* (St. Louis: Historical Publishing Co., 1894). The Mitchell Wolfson Jr. Collection, The Wolfsonian-Florida International University.

together…This was the first time in the history of American art that an opportunity of the kind was afforded them…"[17] Some, however, criticized the architects of the World's Columbian Exposition for relying on European models rather than developing a new American paradigm to suit the occasion.[18] In turn, the Chicago

[11] *Conkey's Complete Guide to the World's Columbian Exposition* (Chicago: W.B. Conkey Company, 1893), 36.

[12] *Conkey's Complete Guide*, 21.

[13] Badger, *The Great American Fair*, xi-xiii.

[14] Rydell, "Rediscovering the 1893 Chicago World's Columbian Exposition," 38.

[15] John J. Flinn, *The Best Things to Be Seen at the World's Fair* (Chicago: The Columbian Guide Company, 1893), 13-20.

[16] Rydell, "Rediscovering the 1893 Chicago World's Columbian Exposition," 20, 25; and R. Reid Badger, "Chicago 1893: World's Columbian Exposition" in John E. Findling, ed., *Historical Dictionary of World's Fairs and Expositions* (New York: Greenwood Press, 1990), 127.

[17] Flinn, 28.

[18] William Walton, *World's Columbian Exposition: Art and Architecture* (Philadelphia: George Barrie, 1893), Volume I, xxi-xxii.

world's fair is generally credited, or blamed, for the predominance of Classicism in American public architecture and urban planning through the 1930s. In what is referred to as the City Beautiful Movement, Daniel Burnham alone designed Beaux Arts plans for Chicago, Washington, San Francisco, and Cleveland, while like-minded peers transformed the face of other American cities.[19] As Hubert Howe Bancroft, a chronicler of the World's Columbian Exposition, summarized: "If for science and industry an historical panorama like this does so much, for art and the cultivation of the beautiful it will do more. The Exhibition itself, and taken as a whole, is a work of art."[20] In all respects, the Chicago world's fair was the ultimate expression of the late-nineteenth-century blossoming of commerce and culture known as the American Renaissance.

The Tiffany Glass and Decorating Company exhibited in the Manufactures and Liberal Arts Building, a mammoth structure on a prominent lake-front site (fig. 68). Both for its size and the extraordinary diversity of its exhibits, the Manufactures and Liberal Arts Building was deemed "perhaps the object the most eagerly sought for by a majority of sight-

seers…"[21] Some commentators considered the building the most severely Classical at the fair,[22] but all commentators, both official and otherwise, did not fail to note the structure's staggering size. The construction of the building required seventeen million feet of lumber, twelve million pounds of steel in the trusses of the central hall, and two million pounds of iron in the roof of the nave; and it cost $1.7 million to construct.[23]

The monolithic, pristine exterior of this behemoth belied the chaotic diversity of the international marketplace within, which displayed the industrial and decorative arts of all participating nations. Photographs of the interior reveal a staggering array of freestanding pavilions that belonged to both corporate and national exhibitors (figs. 69, 70). Commentators described the space with obvious admiration. One opined that the spectator's "impression will be that he is in fairyland, or at least that he is visiting a city of palaces, temples, castles, arches, monuments, and hanging gardens."[24] Exhibits covered the ground floor and the fifty-foot-wide gallery, which ran the perimeter of the building. A small portion of the structure was dedicated to the Liberal Arts Department, an entirely separate division. On the ground floor, the fifty-foot-wide Columbia Avenue ran the length of the building, bisected at perpendicular angles by another broad avenue. Several narrower walkways crossed both of these primary thoroughfares at right angles.[25] More than fifty

68. The Manufactures and Liberal Arts Building. From Hubert Howe Bancroft, *The Book of the Fair* (Chicago and San Francisco: The Bancroft Company, Publishers, 1893). The Mitchell Wolfson Jr. Collection, The Wolfsonian-Florida International University.

19 Badger, "Chicago 1893: World's Columbian Exposition," 130-31.

20 Hubert Howe Bancroft, *The Book of the Fair* (Chicago and San Francisco: The Bancroft Company, Publishers, 1893), 4.

21 Benjamin C. Truman, *History of the World's Fair, Being a Complete and Authentic Description of the Columbian Exposition from Its Inception* (Philadelphia: Mammoth Publishing Co., 1893; New York: rpt. Arno Press, 1976), 209.

22 For example, Flinn, 84.

23 Moses Purnell Handy, ed., *World's Columbian Exposition Official Catalogue* (Chicago: W.B. Conkey Company, 1893), Part VIII, 3.

24 Truman, 210.

69. Interior, east side of the Manufactures and Liberal Arts Building. From J.W. Buel, *The Magic City: A Massive Portfolio of Original Photographic Views of the Great World's Fair* (St. Louis Historical Publishing Co., 1894). The Mitchell Wolfson Jr. Collection, The Wolfsonian-Florida International University.

70. Interior of the Manufactures Department, with clock tower (left of center). From A. Witteman, *The World's Fair* (New York: The Albertype Co., 1893). The Mitchell Wolfson Jr. Collection, The Wolfsonian-Florida International University.

countries were represented in the Manufactures Department, including most of the European nations, several Asian nations (e.g., India, Japan, China, and Siam), and several nations of the Western Hemisphere (e.g., Canada, Mexico, Argentina, Brazil, and Uruguay). But despite this broad representation by other countries, the department had a patently American orientation. According to *The Official Directory*: "It is hoped that every American exhibitor will keep before him the fact that he has not only his own reputation, but that of his country in his

keeping. His product is placed here to challenge comparison and competition with the best that the civilized world can present in the same line."[26] American exhibitions dominated the department, occupying approximately one-third of the floor space; but apparently demand was so great that even American exhibitors were granted only 10 percent of the space for which they applied.[27]

Exhibits were organized by nation and categorized into groups "representing the products of the modern machinery and man's skillful handiwork in many forms and designs."[28] Throughout the World's Columbian Exposition, classifications were based on the distinct segregation of "high art" and "low art" and of production by men and women, so not all of the arts and handicrafts on view at the fair were included in the Manufactures Department. Painting, sculpture, prints, and architecture were exhibited in the Fine Arts Palace; while both the "fine art" and "decorative art" produced by women were exhibited in the Woman's Building. Many of the classification groups in the Manufactures Department—such as those comprising chemicals, weapons and ammunition, refrigerators, and hardware—were technical in nature and had little or nothing to do with the decorative arts or design. There were, however, a great number of groups that presented objects associated with the arts and crafts industries. The nine consecutive groups numbered 90–98, in particular, included such products as furniture, upholstery, ceramics, mosaics, monuments, mantels, art metalwork, glassware, stained glass, carvings, gold and silverware, and jewelry. *The Official Catalogue* reveals that Tiffany Glass and Decorating Company registered objects in eight of these nine groups, having abstained only from Group 97, which featured gold and silverware. In

[25] Flinn, 83.

[26] Moses Purnell Handy, *The Official Directory of the World's Columbian Exposition, May 1st to October 30th, 1893* (Chicago: W.B. Conkey Company, 1893), 223.

[27] Bancroft, 142.

[28] Handy, *The Official Directory of the World's Columbian Exposition*, 223.

addition, the firm registered in three other categories: Group 114 (lighting), Group 117 (wire goods, screens, latticework), and Group 118 (wrought iron).[29]

The majority of American manufacturers exhibited their products in areas dedicated to a specific type of object. For example, virtually all of the American exhibitors in Group 95, "Stained Glass in Decoration," showed their wares in the northeast corner of the building's second-floor gallery.[30] While Tiffany Glass and Decorating Company registered objects in many different categories, the firm exhibited all of its products in a single location. This space was located at the physical and symbolic center of the Manufactures and Liberal Arts Building, adjacent to and generally considered part of the exhibit pavilion of Tiffany & Co., the firm of Louis Comfort Tiffany's father. Tiffany & Co. was granted a prominent location at the intersection of Columbia Avenue and its bisecting walkway, on the northeast corner of the 125-foot-high electric clock tower that served as the fair's official timepiece (fig 71).[31] The other three corners of the electric clock provided access to the exhibits of France, Great Britain, and Germany. The cream-colored and gold-ornamented pavilion occupied jointly by Tiffany & Co. and Gorham Manufacturing Company marked one's passage into the host country's section. Signage on a tall, fluted Doric column at the pavilion's front proclaimed: "The United States of America Bids the Whole World Welcome."

Adjacent to this pavilion, Tiffany Glass and Decorating Company mounted an ambitious tripartite exhibition, consisting of the chapel and the Dark Room and Light Room. Patricia Pongracz Spicka has established that the chapel, the largest of the spaces, was installed in a simple rectangular edifice, brandishing on its exterior the firm's name and a large figural banner featuring the Virgin and Child.[32] The exhibition was described in a promotional brochure by the Tiffany Glass and Decorating Company and in other accounts of the fair. With its prominent arches and chromatic exuberance, the chapel was variously seen as a Byzantine or Romanesque confection.[33] The character of the chapel is described in detail in the chapter "A Tiffany Masterpiece Rediscovered" in this book.

The Dark Room and the Light Room, though not associated with a specific program or function, were two salons of a residential character. Together, they showcased the Tiffany Glass and Decorating Company's secular products. The Dark Room was a compellingly unified study in the color green, its contents all ranging from yellow-green to blue-green in tone, including the oak beam ceiling. The furnishings comprised a quartered-oak table with a green leather cover, a bench of wood mosaic, green leather curtains, and a gilded chair and sofa upholstered in yellow silk with green velvet. Most prominent was a hooded mantle, surrounded by a marble and inlaid-glass border and flanked by royal green marble seats. On the other side of a heavy tapestry curtain was the Light Room, a study in pale, iridescent tones. The silvery ceiling, studded with opal and turquoise jewels, set the theme. The

---

29 Information derived from departmental listing of exhibitors in Handy, ed., *World's Columbian Exposition Official Catalogue*, Part VIII, 8-9, 24-29, 42, 46-47.

30 It should be noted that, according to a site plan (see Bancroft, 55), some industrial exhibitors eschewed the Manufactures and Liberal Arts Building entirely, choosing instead to show their product on the Midway Plaisance. Those of particular relevance to the Tiffany Glass and Decorating Company included Bohemian Glass Company, Libbey Glass Company, and Venice Murano Company, all of which presumably found the popular exposure of the Midway irresistible.

31 Bancroft, 142-45.

32 Spicka, "The Installation of the Tiffany Chapel at the World's Columbian Exposition, Jackson Park, Chicago, 1893," unpublished, October 15, 1996, "Addendum," 1.

33 Truman, 219; McKean, 56-59.

71. Tiffany & Co. pavilion in the Manufactures Department. From C.D. Arnold and H.D. Higinbotham, *Official Views of the World's Columbian Exposition* (Chicago: Press Chicago Photo-Gravure Co., 1893). The Mitchell Wolfson Jr. Collection, The Wolfsonian-Florida International University.

firm's *Synopsis of the Exhibit* brochure refers to only two components of the Light Room's furnishings: an electric light and two stained-glass windows. The light was composed of metal and mother-of-pearl, and prefigured the firm's phenomenal success with decorative lamps. The windows demonstrated the potential for non-biblical representations in stained glass. One portrayed parakeets resting in a blossoming fruit tree from which a bowl of goldfish was suspended; the other represented a woman feeding flamingos in the court of a Roman-style house (fig. 72).[34] In their apparent absence of narrative and their focus on beauty, both reflect the "art-for-art's-sake" attitude of the Aesthetic Movement.

Despite these lavish exhibits, historians have suggested that Louis Comfort Tiffany was somewhat reluctant to present his decorative work at the World's Columbian Exposition. In *Louis C. Tiffany: Rebel in Glass*, for example, Robert Koch maintained that Paris-based gallery owner Siegfried Bing, who played a major role in promoting Tiffany throughout Europe, was largely responsible for convincing the American designer to participate in Chicago. Koch also noted that the firm's exhibit was not complete by the opening of the fair.[35] Official publications confirm that the Tiffany Glass and Decorating Company subscribed to the Manufactures Department late in the process. In an early version of the world's fair catalogue, the firm

[34] Tiffany Glass and Decorating Company, *A Synopsis of the Exhibit of the Tiffany Glass and Decorating Company in the American Section of the Manufactures and Liberal Arts Building at the World's Fair, Jackson Park, Chicago, Illinois, 1893, with an Appendix on Memorial Windows* (New York, 1893), 4-8.

[35] Koch, 75.

72. Louis Comfort Tiffany. Tiffany Glass and Decorating Company. *Feeding the Flamingos*, ca. 1892. Leaded Favrile glass, 61 x 45 in. (156.8 x 115.6 cm). Morse Museum of American Art (U-072).

was not included in the alphabetical exhibitors' lists at all.[36] Given that Tiffany had already exhibited paintings at expositions in Philadelphia and Paris, it is difficult to understand why this savvy businessman would have delayed his participation or considered abstaining from the even-more-ambitious 1893 fair.

Evidence suggests that Tiffany was dissatisfied with the physical conditions or perhaps the classification system of the Manufactures Department at the World's Columbian Exposition, particularly as they pertained to the exhibition of stained glass. In an article on America's contribution to the burgeoning field of stained glass, published in the July 1893 issue of *The Forum*, Tiffany contended:

you will look in vain in the great "White City" on the shores of Lake Michigan for a department in the Exposition devoted exclusively to exhibiting the results of the development in this particular art. This is the more to be regretted as in a new art such as this exhibitions are of great use; the artist comes face to face with his fellow-artists, and patrons are better able to judge of the merits of the work of each. Moreover, an intelligent exhibition would have aided greatly in crushing out the purely commercial spirit which too often invades this field, while the American people as well as European visitors of taste and discernment would have been aroused to the important strides made in this direction.[37]

Tiffany was exaggerating, for, as explained above, Group 95 in the Manufactures Department

was dedicated exclusively to the medium of stained glass, and it attracted approximately ten exhibitors. Though his argument was flawed, Tiffany apparently embraced it for years to come. The same accusation reappeared almost verbatim in the 1914 authorized biography of Tiffany by Charles de Kay, who stated: "the managers of the World's Fair at Chicago had not made provision for showing American windows." That Tiffany's grievance was actually based on the quality and perhaps the quantity—rather than the absence—of exhibit space for stained glass is subsequently suggested by de Kay. In a more objective critique of the World's Columbian Exposition later in his book, he added: "the managers of such fairs declined the expense of preparing suitable halls with day and night lighting such as are needed for the proper exhibition of stained glass. They are indeed unwieldy objects to exhibit."[38] In *The "Lost" Treasures of Louis Comfort Tiffany*, Hugh McKean reinforced the perception that "no provisions had been made to exhibit leaded windows" at the World's Columbian Exposition.[39]

The chapel and the firm's other exhibits were, to some extent, incongruous additions to the World's Columbian Exposition, perhaps further explaining the Tiffany Glass and Decorating Company's possible ambivalence about the project. While the world's fair celebrated a rediscovery of Classical civilization in its art and architecture, Tiffany's chapel and stained glass were both inspired by traditions associated with the Middle Ages. The intimately scaled, nostalgic, and ecclesiastically inspired Tiffany Chapel was, likewise, an incongruity within the Manufactures Department, which was characterized by its vast size, a commitment to technological progress, and a focus on consumerism. Hugh McKean discerned the unusual character of Tiffany's chapel in the world's fair context,

---

36 In the final version, Tiffany Glass and Decorating Company's exhibits were, in some instances, assigned numbers abandoned by earlier subscribers and, in other instances, assigned numbers added to the sequence (e.g., "283a"). See Handy, *The Official Directory of the World's Columbian Exposition*, 241-44; and Handy, ed., *World's Columbian Exposition Official Catalogue*, Part VIII, 8-9, 24-29, 42, 46-47.

37 Louis Comfort Tiffany, "American Art Supreme in Colored Glass," *The Forum* (July 1893), 621.

38 [Charles de Kay], *The Art Work of Louis C. Tiffany* (1914; rpt. Poughkeepsie: Apollo, 1987), 20, 25.

39 McKean, 4-5.

describing it along with Adler and Sullivan's portal for the Transportation Building as "two exceptions to all the plaster classicism" (fig. 73).[40] One other notable exception was the reproduction of the Franciscan monastery of La Rábida, erected by the World's Columbian Exposition's board of directors. Columbus reputedly took refuge at the original monastery "in the hour of his greatest need."[41] The reproduction in Jackson Park housed Columbus memorabilia. As a medieval-inspired structure with ecclesiastical associations, but not an ecclesiastical function, the prominent La Rábida exhibit may be seen as a symbolic companion to the Tiffany Chapel. The Adler and Sullivan building and La Rábida notwithstanding, the Tiffany exhibits contrasted greatly with the White City's dominant Classical aesthetic.

Ultimately, though, Tiffany used the World's Columbian Exposition to his great advantage. By arguing that there were no stained-glass exhibits at the 1893 world's fair, Tiffany, intentionally or not, legitimized his decision to present all of his products in a single exhibition, rather than breaking them up by classification. In so doing, Tiffany further established his reputation as the preeminent designer of stained glass in America, built his ecclesiastical market, promoted the diversity of his work as an all-around designer, and built his credibility among affluent prospective clients. These conclusions are supported by further analysis of the Tiffany Glass and Decorating Company's 1893 exhibition and of two pivotal publications: Louis Comfort Tiffany's July 1893 article in *The Forum* entitled "American Art Supreme in Colored Glass," and his firm's *Synopsis* of its 1893 exhibits.

First and foremost, Tiffany utilized the World's Columbian Exposition to establish his reputation as

73. Adler and Sullivan's Transportation Building. From Halsey C. Ives, *The Dream City* (St. Louis: N.D. Thompson Publishing Co., 1893). The Mitchell Wolfson Jr. Collection, The Wolfsonian-Florida International University.

the world's preeminent designer of glass. By 1893, the Tiffany Glass and Decorating Company had already executed a large number of stained-glass windows for churches and other edifices in the United States. However, many of America's wealthier individuals and institutions still preferred to import their art and stained glass from Europe.[42] The World's Columbian Exposition was meant to showcase American progress in the arts and industry. This was a fitting objective for a fair dedicated to Columbus, the man symbolically credited with putting the "New World" on the "Old World's" map. In this spirit, Tiffany began his article on stained glass in *The Forum* with a bold assertion:

Walter Savage Landor, it is said, would not visit America because there was no stained-glass to be seen here. Since the eccentric Englishman made this remark, great changes have taken place, and to-day this country unquestionably leads the world in the production of colored glass windows of artistic value and decorative importance.[43]

Later in the same essay, Tiffany explained that the American stained-glass tradition was based on achieving color and depth through mosaic rather than paint. This practice was amply demonstrated in his stained-

[40] McKean, 5.

[41] J.W. Buel, *The Magic City: A Massive Portfolio of Original Photographic Views of the Great World's Fair* (St. Louis: Historical Publishing Co., 1894), np.

[42] Koch, 78.

[43] Tiffany, 621.

glass work at the World's Columbian Exposition. Pointing out various late-nineteenth-century American innovations in the field, particularly the layering of colored glass, Tiffany further declared, "I maintain that the best American colored windows are superior to the best mediaeval windows."[44] By claiming both the superiority of nineteenth-century American stained glass in the history of the world and the absence of American stained glass at the 1893 exposition, Tiffany effectively positioned his own exhibits as the finest at the fair, and hence the finest in the world. As the medium's self-appointed spokesperson in *The Forum*, Tiffany strove to identify his firm as the dominant producers of stained glass. Ironically, Tiffany's chief competitor, John La Farge, had already garnered critical acclaim for opalescent American stained glass at the Paris Exposition of 1889.[45] It would thus seem that Tiffany viewed the World's Columbian Exposition as a chance to establish the preeminence of his own contributions. Not surprisingly, La Farge issued a swift rebuttal to the *Forum* article,[46] but following the 1893 exhibit his reputation would soon be dwarfed by Tiffany's.

In *The Forum*, Tiffany also aimed to foster appreciation of American stained glass as a fine art rather than a commercial art, noting: "An American window cannot be left in the hands of an artisan if the desire is to produce a successful work of art."[47] At the World's Columbian Exposition, the stained-glass

medium was firmly relegated to the Manufactures Department; however, Tiffany was recognized as a "fine artist" through the inclusion of his watercolors and oil paintings in the Palace of Fine Arts.[48] By literally separating his stained glass from that of the other stained-glass exhibitors in Group 95, though, Tiffany figuratively separated his work as well. Rather than exhibiting alongside an entourage of stained-glass manufacturers, Tiffany could distance himself from a *craft* practice and emerge, refashioned, as the nation's preeminent stained-glass *artist*. Elizabeth Johnston De Rosa notes that Tiffany attempted to "cultivate the romantic theme that he was a lone genius expressing his personal vision through his art."[49] By presenting his windows apart from those of the other stained-glass manufacturers, Tiffany gave physical expression to this fantasy, suggesting that his work emanated not from an artisan tradition practiced by many others, but as a wholly independent act of creative inspiration. Identifying himself as an aesthete rather than a craftsman, Tiffany was ultimately a perfect fit for the fair that strove to impart beauty to daily life.

In conjunction with these efforts to establish his preeminence as an artist in stained glass, Tiffany also took the opportunity to develop his firm's reputation as leading providers of ecclesiastical fittings in glass and other materials. After the Civil War, the Second Great Awakening caused a surge in church-building across the United States. To support the burden of this expense, congregations encouraged members to memorialize their loved ones by donating portions of the buildings, altars, pews, fonts, and other ecclesiastical furnishings, most notably stained-glass windows.[50] The Tiffany Glass and Decorating Company's 1893 *Synopsis* demonstrates the extent to which the firm had already participated in church

---

44 Tiffany, 623-26.

45 Herwin Schaefer, "Tiffany's Fame in Europe," *The Art Bulletin 44* (December 1962), 311.

46 La Farge's Booklet is referenced by Koch, 79.

47 Tiffany, 627.

48 Handy, ed., *World's Columbian Exposition Official Catalogue*, Part X, 27, 33. According to this source, Tiffany exhibited six watercolors and two paintings in oil.

49 Elizabeth Johnson De Rosa, *Louis Comfort Tiffany and the Development of Religious Landscape Memorial Windows* (Ann Arbor: UMI Dissertation Services, 1995), 29.

50 De Rosa, 14-15, 23.

74. Exhibition of Hems and Sons in the Manufactures Department. From J.W. Buel, *The Magic City: A Massive Portfolio of Original Photographic Views of the Great World's Fair* (St. Louis: Historical Publishing Co., 1894). The Mitchell Wolfson Jr. Collection, The Wolfsonian-Florida International University.

projects across the United States, its Appendix listing approximately 240 executed memorial windows in twenty-four states and the District of Columbia.[51]

Alice Cooney Frelinghuysen has noted that the World's Columbian Exposition chapel served as a showroom for the full range of ecclesiastical designs produced by the Tiffany Glass and Decorating Company.[52] The firm's demonstration of its dexterity and diversity in church-related products was made possible by the fact that it exhibited all of its ecclesiastical wares in one location rather than scattering them into several exhibitions by object classification or group. In this respect, the Tiffany Chapel is analogous to other exhibits, such as that by Hems and Sons, a British firm that presented church fittings and ecclesi-

astical artwork elsewhere in the Manufactures Department (fig.74). According to contemporary commentator J.W. Buel, the Hems and Sons display "was one of the sights of the exhibition toward which devout visitors turned again and again…"[53] It is probable that the chapel was likewise a popular destination for the "devout visitor," and a major attraction during the September 1893 World's Parliament of Religions congress.[54] But relative to the Hems and Sons exhibit and others like it, the Tiffany Chapel had distinct advantages. Patricia Pongracz Spicka has pointed out that, by presenting his ecclesiastical furnishings in an environment that evoked religious authenticity, Tiffany created a space that visitors seem to have experienced as moving and spiritual. Moreover, unlike other eccle-

[51] Tiffany Glass and Decorating Company, 30-32.

[52] Frelinghuysen, 22.

[53] Buel, np.

[54] The World's Parliament of Religions is discussed by Badger, "Chicago 1893: World's Columbian Exposition," 130.

marble and glass mosaics, wood-carving and inlaying, metal work, embroideries, upholsteries, and hangings.[55]

siastical exhibits, those of the Tiffany Glass and Decorating Company were complemented by the secular items in the Dark Room and the Light Room. While the chapel itself would have attracted those specifically interested in religious material goods, the decorative salons would have attracted wealthy patrons interested primarily in residential material goods, but also in the habit of sponsoring memorial windows and other furnishings for their growing congregations. Although the firm's ecclesiastical and secular exhibits seem somewhat disconnected at first, they likely functioned as symbiotic components of client cultivation.

Louis Comfort Tiffany's decision to integrate objects from eleven different categories into one exhibition that was both sacred and secular also demonstrated the firm's commitment to and expertise in creating complete and unified design environments of every variety. In effect, the Tiffany Glass and Decorating Company's exhibition offered one-stop decorative shopping that would not have been possible with physically segregated, object-specific exhibits. The firm's *Synopsis* of its 1893 exhibits opened with a pointed declaration of this objective:

We have endeavored, in our exhibit, to bring before the eyes of the visitors to the World's Fair various objects from different departments in order to illustrate the scope of our business, which embraces all forms of ecclesiastical and domestic embellishment. It will be seen from our exhibit that there is hardly a material known to the decorator but what we employ in our work, and that, in fact, we cover the whole field of decoration—frescoes and mural paintings, colored glass windows,

In claiming to offer just about everything, the Tiffany Glass and Decorating Company represented itself as a microcosm of the entire Manufactures Department in which it was housed. Moreover, in its expression of unified design, the Tiffany exhibit acted as interior analogue to the laboriously unified art and architecture program of the White City, albeit in a starkly different aesthetic.

The design concept known as *Gesamtkunstwerk* (complete design unity) is central to the Arts and Crafts Movement and dominated Tiffany's high-end interior decoration of the 1880s, including such projects as the Henry Osborne and Louisine Havemeyer residence in New York and the redesign of the White House for President Chester Arthur. It is evident that by 1893, with such illustrious commissions behind him, Tiffany was firmly ensconced as a master of this practice. As unified suites on a domestic scale, the Dark Room and Light Room referenced these landmark residential achievements, while the chapel revealed the firm's substantial capacity for bringing unified design to church interiors. That Tiffany's recognition as a designer of unified secular interiors was used to foster comparable ecclesiastical commissions is suggested by the format of the *Synopsis* brochure. Following a brief introduction, the promotional document leads the visitor through the Dark Room and the Light Room, and then concludes in the chapel. On paper, at least, the secular *Gesamtkunstwerk* paved the way for sacred equivalents. Whether this followed the actual sequence of one's visit or not, the *Synopsis* did reflect the firm's movement toward ecclesiastical products in the 1890s.

[55] Tiffany Glass and Decorating Company, 3. This quotation similarly appears in Spicka, as evidence of the breadth and decorative principles of Tiffany Glass and Decorating Company.

By integrating an array of objects into a single exhibition, the Tiffany Glass and Decorating Company solidified its reputation for stained-glass windows, demonstrated its capacity to design ecclesiastical furnishings, and brought attention to its unified interiors. Although their design significance is clear, the 1893 exhibits can be seen as a carefully choreographed initiative to expand the firm's client base. This was also the impact of the firm's decision to exhibit in a portion of the Tiffany & Co. pavilion. Though this proximity might have resulted from Louis Comfort Tiffany's belated entry into the World's Columbian Exposition, the close relationship between the two Tiffany exhibits merits consideration. Most obviously, by exhibiting alongside Tiffany & Co., the Tiffany Glass and Decorating Company secured an unusually prominent position, in the dead center of the Manufactures Department, at the gateway to the American exhibits. Acknowledging the advantage of this situation, commentator Benjamin Truman wrote: "Of course, every one who visits the Manufactures Building has seen the Tiffany pavilion, with its tall, eagle-tipped tower."[56] World's fair chronicler Hubert Howe Bancroft noted that Tiffany and Gorham had been given "one of the places of honor" on the condition that they "do credit to the nation and to themselves."[57]

The Tiffany & Co. exhibits were extremely lavish and the general consensus of critics was that the firm had fulfilled all expectations. John Flinn waxed effusive in his description of the jewelry firm's pavilion:

No private pavilion at this or any other international exposition was ever constructed upon a scale so expensive and costly. But the exhibits it contains are even more worthy of special mention and attention. Inside the Tiffany pavilion there is unquestionably the most costly display of jewelry and precious stones ever made.[58]

Throughout his career, Louis Comfort Tiffany enjoyed capital, clients, legitimacy, and prestige through association with his father's successful New York firm.[59] The World's Columbian Exposition undoubtedly proved no exception to this familial tradition. Tiffany & Co.'s ostentatious display attracted great admiration and notoriety, for it included a more-than-125-carat diamond, an incense burner in the shape of a duck being strangled by a rattlesnake, and an Indian chrysanthemum dinner set of six hundred pieces.[60] Moving from the father's space to the son's, Benjamin Truman remarked: "The Tiffany Glass and Decorating Company has not so costly an exhibit, but it is quite as artistic and beautiful."[61] One can hypothesize that Louis Comfort Tiffany's firm would have appealed to and benefited from visitors attracted by the magnificence of his father's pavilion. The two firms again exhibited side-by-side at the Paris Exposition of 1900,[62] demonstrating that Louis Comfort Tiffany recognized the benefit of such proximity.

The fact that Tiffany had already executed important commissions for some of America's most prominent citizens and scores of churches by 1893 hints that the impact of the World's Columbian

[56] Truman, 217.
[57] Bancroft, 147.
[58] Flinn, 92-93.
[59] See, for example, Neil Harris, "Louis Comfort Tiffany: The Search for Influence," in *Masterworks of Louis Comfort Tiffany*, 16.
[60] Truman, 217; and Bancroft, 148.
[61] Truman, 219.
[62] Diane Chalmers Johnson, *American Art Nouveau* (New York: Harry N. Abrams, 1981), 37.

exhibits may have been overstated, most notably by the artist himself.

In several respects, though, the 1893 world's fair satisfied Tiffany's promotional objectives. The *Synopsis* brochure and his article in *The Forum* document Tiffany's ability to use the fair as a marketing vehicle. While several of the comprehensive illustrated accounts of the 1893 world's fair make incomplete mention or no mention of the Tiffany Glass and Decorating Company exhibition,[63] in many instances it would seem that Louis Comfort Tiffany's exhibits and his rhetoric worked with mesmerizing efficacy. An October 1893 article in *The Decorator and Furnisher*, for example, offered a lengthy description of the chapel and the decorated salons, repeating the Tiffany Glass and Decorating Company's *Synopsis* almost verbatim, and treating Louis Comfort Tiffany's self-aggrandizing assertions as hard facts.[64] Elizabeth Johnston De Rosa has postulated that Tiffany's skillful self-promotion was partly responsible for the assessment that his technical innovations constituted an entirely new school of stained glass.[65]

While previous accounts might not have considered the exact means by which Tiffany used the fair to promote the work of Tiffany Glass and Decorating Company, there is good reason to accept their conclu-

sions about the importance of the World's Columbian Exposition in the artist's career. Louis Comfort Tiffany was awarded fifty-four honorary medals in Chicago, and it is estimated that about one and a half million people visited his firm's exhibition there.[66] To keep up with increased orders following the fair, it is said that Tiffany retained the staff he had hired to construct the 1893 chapel.[67] Obviously recognizing the value of international expositions, Tiffany subsequently participated in the Paris, Buffalo, Turin, and St. Louis world's fairs between 1900 and 1904.[68] A compelling analysis by Herwin Schaefer specifically documents how the World's Columbian exhibits stimulated the market for Tiffany in Europe. Schaefer explains that, in the years immediately following the 1893 world's fair, Tiffany's work was purchased by museums in London, Paris, Vienna, and Berlin.[69]

And while Tiffany was arguably in the domestic limelight before the fair, Chicago either foreshadowed or partially fostered his meteoric ascent and expansion in the United States as well. The electric light fixture he exhibited in 1893, for example, may be seen as a harbinger of his later serial- and mass-production lamps. Interestingly, though, 1893 also marked the year in which Tiffany established his own glass-making plant in Corona, Queens, New York. There, the firm produced Favrile glass and, from it, an array of small artistic objects, such as vases and bowls. These would dominate the Tiffany Glass and Decorating Company's exhibition at the Paris Exposition of 1900, and earn the firm its greatest renown.[70] Surprisingly, they are not even mentioned in Tiffany-generated material surrounding the landmark exhibit at the World's Columbian Exposition.[71]

[63] See, for example, Buel.

[64] "Tiffany Glass and Decorating Company's Exhibit at the Columbian Exposition," The Decorator and Furnisher 23 (October 1893), 9-11.

[65] De Rosa, 23.

[66] Koch, 107; and McKean, 137-38.

[67] Koch, 78.

[68] Frelinghuysen, 4.

[69] See Schaefer, 309-28.

[70] Koch, 120.

[71] Favrile glass articles are not mentioned in The Synopsis or The Forum article. Most sources indicate that Favrile glass articles were not exhibited until 1894 (see, for example, Schaefer and Frelinghuysen). In the firm's promotional brochure for the 1900 Paris world's fair it is noted that blown glass articles were first exhibited in 1893, but the location at which they were shown is not specified. See Tiffany Studios Allied Arts Company, The Exhibit of Louis C. Tiffany from the Tiffany Studios, 333 to 341 Fourth Avenue, New York...Exposition Universelle, Paris, 1900 (New York: Tiffany Studios Allied Arts Company, 1900), np.

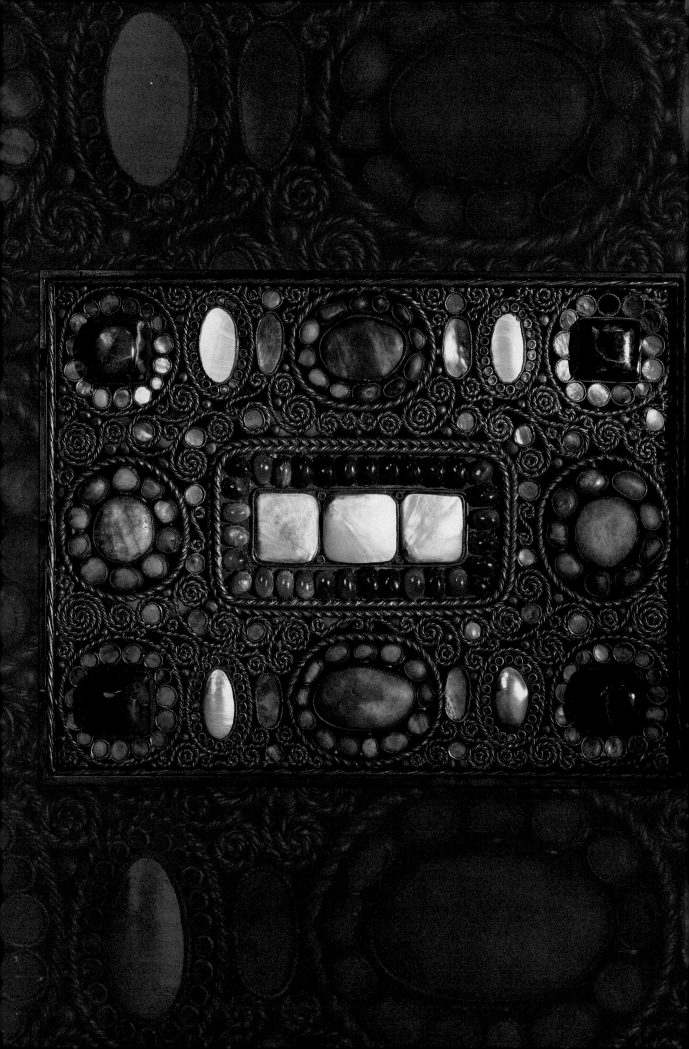

THE CHAPEL'S FIRST INSTALLATION and Move to Saint John the Divine

by PATRICIA PONGRACZ SPICKA

Tiffany Glass and Decorating Company occupied an exhibition space in Section N, Block 1, in the American Division of the Manufactures and Liberal Arts Building (fig. 75) at the World's Columbian Exposition. Louis Comfort Tiffany's display of ecclesiastic furnishings and stained-glass windows was exhibited with "gold, silver and plated ware," and "jewelry and ornaments" adjacent to his father's exhibition for Tiffany & Co. and that of Gorham and Company.

To understand the significance of the location of the Tiffany Glass and Decorating Company's exhibition space, a brief discussion of the general plan of exhibitions in the Manufactures and Liberal Arts Building is useful. The official guide to the World's Columbian Exposition touts the building as "the largest in the world, and is the largest under one roof ever erected."[1] Designed by architect George B. Post of New York, the rectangular building measured 1,687 by 787 feet, its walls rose to a height of 66 feet, and the roof over its center hall rose to 237.6 feet.[2] The interior of the building was divided into a "great central hall" measuring 380 by 1,280 feet, which was surrounded by a nave 107 feet wide. The central hall and nave were further augmented by a surrounding gallery measuring 50 feet.[3] The sheer size of this space is best indicated by a guide to the exposition which described the central hall, where the Tiffany Glass and Decorating Company displayed its chapel, as:

a single room without a supporting pillar under its roof, has a floor a fraction less than eleven acres, and 75,000 persons can sit in this room, giving each one six square feet of space. By the same arrangement, the entire building will seat 300,000 people. It is theoretically possible to mobilize the entire standing Army of Russia under its roof. [4]

To aid the visitor in experiencing the spectacle in this massive building, the exhibits were organized according to classification: "Group 95 Stained Glass in Decoration,"[5] "Group 89 Typewriters, Paper, Blank Books, Stationery,"[6] etc., and the exhibits were laid out on a grid of streets named in honor of the exposition.

---

[1] World's Columbian Exposition, 1893, Official Guide Catalogue, Part VII. Manufactures and Liberal Arts Building, Leather and Shoe Building, Department H. Manufactures (Chicago: W.B. Conkey, 1893), 3.
[2] Ibid.
[3] Ibid.
[4] Ibid.

The chapel installation stood on the corner of Columbia Avenue in a simple rectangular edifice, and the baptistery was contained in the smaller building attached to the south face of the chapel edifice (see fig. 16). Unfortunately, no photographs of the interior of the chapel as it appeared at the exposition of 1893 are known to exist; one illustration of the chapel interior is a chromolithograph of a watercolor after Joseph Lauber in the collection of the Morse Museum of American Art (see fig. 15). The interior of the chapel may be approximated further when the watercolor is viewed in conjunction with a pamphlet published by the Tiffany Glass and Decorating Company.[7]

The Tiffany Glass and Decorating Company viewer's guide illustrates that the chapel exhibition was conceived as an architectural setting for the display of a range of liturgical furnishings and objects. The guide indicates that the goals of the Tiffany Glass and Decorating Company's exhibition were to illustrate both the breadth of works it produced, "which embraces all forms of ecclesiastical and domestic embellishment," and the decorative principles understood by the company's decorators on display in the Dark Room, the Light Room, and the chapel settings designed for the fair.[8]

The description, a discursive list of the decorative components of the chapel, illustrates that the objects on display were of primary importance. The visitor was guided to look at the altar, retables, tabernacle, candlesticks, altar cross, etc., and not at the walls, floor or ceiling, which were neither described nor mentioned in any detail.

As it appeared in Chicago, the chapel was a richly decorated, small yet monumental space. Though the chapel building was small, the form and materials contained within invited compari-

75. Above: Charles Graham, artist. Manufactures and Liberal Arts Building at World's Columbian Exposition, Chicago, 1893. Chicago Historical Society (g1943.17).

76. Next page, top: Detail of *Tiffany Chapel Altar*, St John. Marble, glass, and mother-of-pearl.

77. Next page, bottom: Detail of *Tiffany Chapel Altar*, St. Matthew.

son with medieval proto-
types. The mosaic-encrusted
altar was raised on a marble
predella, a stepped platform, with
mosaic risers. The altar front depicted the Chi Ro, Christ's symbol, inscribed
in a circle flanked by the symbols of the four evangelists (figs. 76, 77, 78, 79). Set upon the altar's marble top was a golden jeweled tabernacle contained
within retables, raised steps on top of the altar. Set
upon the uppermost retable was a gold-and-jewel-
encrusted cross, now lost, flanked by two gold fili-
gree and jewel-encrusted candlesticks containing
electrified candles. Above and behind the altar was a
mosaic reredos, a semi-circular panel, depicting a
jeweled crown, a serpentine vine and two peacocks;
the iridescent quality of the purple and golden
mosaic glass described perfectly the luminescence
of peacock feathers.

The entire altar program was set against
twelve receding mosaic columns which supported a
canopy of similarly receding arches above; columns
and arches together created a niche-like frame for
the altar emphasizing both its centrality in the decorative program and its prominence in a sacred
context. Columns punctuated the chapel walls and
were joined by a heavy continuous cornice. The
side walls contained figural windows. The chapel
was illuminated from above by a cruciform electrolier composed of green turtle-back glass tiles. To

one side of the altar a marble and mosaic lectern
stood flanked by two tall
mosaic candlesticks. Seated
within the chapel, the
visitor was contained in a
sturdy, glimmering space
which focused attention on the
altar.

The description of the chapel
suggests that Tiffany Glass and Decorating Company
placed emphases both on the decorative harmony
of objects and on the symbolic meaning of the
liturgical objects it designed. For example, the
description of the reredos illustrates that the designers understood how to work in "polished black
marble and iridescent glass mosaic"; the decorative
effect of the "deep blue and pearl-like lights" these
materials produced on the whole installation; and
the relevance of the design of the vine to the reredos it covered.[9] The description explains the choice
of the vine design, stating:

The design employed is the Vine,
symbolical of the sacrament of
the Eucharist, and among
those vines there are por-
trayed peacocks, used here
after the manner of the
Primitive Christians, as
symbolizing immortality, for
it was believed in the early ages
that the flesh of the peacock was incor-
ruptible. The aim of the designer was two-fold: first to
convey to the minds of the spectators that the joys of
immortality are dependent upon the Vine of the New

[5] Ibid., 9.

[6] Ibid., 7.

[7] Tiffany Glass and Decorating Company, *A Synopsis of the Exhibit of the Tiffany Glass and Decorating Company in the American Section of the Manufactures and Liberal Arts Building at the World's Fair, Jackson Park, Chicago, IL, 1893, with an Appendix on Memorial Windows* (New York: J.J. Little and Co., 1893).

[8] Ibid., 3.

[9] Ibid., 12

Testament, and, secondly, to illustrate by symbols the sacred texts which are inscribed upon the retables. [10]

According to this passage, the design of the vine in "iridescent glass mosaic" was in harmony with the tabernacle door (fig. 80) covered in "semi-precious marbles" and "real gems" and the "gold mosaic" of the retables illustrating in white mosaic letters an inscription from the "sixth chapter of the Gospel, according to St. John, and directly relating to the Eucharistic office." Thus, reredos, retables, and tabernacle (designed to eventually contain the Eucharist) were related decoratively and symbolically. All were encrusted with rich, glittering ornamentation. The vine, symbolic of the Eucharist; the peacocks, symbolic of immortality; and the passages concerning the Eucharist inscribed on the retables, together encouraged viewers to contemplate the immortality that faith—embodied in the Eucharist contained in the tabernacle—would bring. The Tiffany Glass and Decorating Company elided decorative form with liturgical function to create a materially and symbolically complex chapel program.

Tiffany desired to create a suitable context for the display of his company's works. As the *American Architect and Building News* reported on November 11, 1893, the chapel installation achieved the desired effect on visitors to the display. The objects exhibited conveyed to the viewer the range of designs Tiffany Glass and Decorating Company was capable of producing, as the liturgical setting in which the objects were displayed conveyed the

sense that the company knew ultimately for whom and for what type of space it was designing. The article praised the chapel, stating:

Of the work displayed at the Fair, Tiffany's was noticeably the most artistic produced. It is to be regretted that the exhibit of glass as actual works of art was not larger, as it could not have failed to be exceedingly interesting. It certainly would have proved attractive to a great many people if one might judge by the crowds that even in the early part of the Fair season filled to more than overflowing Tiffany's pavilion. [11]

In this passage, Tiffany's chapel installation becomes the standard to which the displays of all the other glass firms are compared. Stating that "Tiffany's was noticeably the most artistic [installation] produced" at the exposition, the article laments that other firms did not display "glass as actual works of art" as did the Tiffany Glass and Decorating Company.

Perhaps the most significant statement of this passage is the reported popularity of the chapel installation with visitors to the fair: Tiffany's pavilion was filled to "overflowing" even early in the fair season. From this report, it appears that critics and

[10] Ibid.

[11] "Chicago-American vs. Foreign Stained Glass," *The American Architect and Building News* XLII (November 1893), 75.

visitors alike were intrigued by the chapel installation; displaying objects in an appropriate setting caught people's eyes. The article continues to describe the chapel, stating:

Tiffany was the only firm that gave its glass any artistic setting. The ecclesiastic glass either for windows or lamps was placed in a Romanesque chapel so perfect in its appointments that it was not an uncommon sight to see men remove their hats upon entering the "sacred" precincts.[12]

The article indicates that the chapel installation, unique among all exhibits on display, inspired interest and even respect in the viewer. This passage indicates that placing the liturgical objects on display in an architectural setting encouraged visitors to interact with the objects displayed in the chapel, rather than viewing them in a case. Visitors to Tiffany's chapel experienced the objects before them and appreciated their significance in a larger worldly context. It was this experience that lead Mrs. Celia Hermoine Whipple Wallace to purchase the World's Columbian Exposition display as a memorial chapel for the Cathedral Church of Saint John the Divine in New York City.[13]

From January 8, 1899 to April 19, 1911 the Tiffany Chapel was the primary consecrated space of the Cathedral Church of Saint John the Divine, 1047 Amsterdam Avenue at 112th Street, New York.

The correspondence concerning Mrs. Wallace's donation of the Tiffany Chapel to the cathedral indicates that the chapel was received with reservation. In a letter dated April 2, 1896, Bishop Henry Codman Potter wrote that:

[12] Ibid.

[13] Cathedral League, *Cathedral Church of Saint John the Divine* (New York: St. Bartholomew's Press, 1916), 22.

[14] Bishop Henry Codman Potter to George MacCulloch Miller, Esq., April 2, 1896, New York.

Mrs. Atwell [it is assumed that Mrs. Atwell represented Mrs. Wallace] of Chicago desires to present to the Cathedral what is known as the Tiffany Chapel, and in order to do so, requests that a plan of the location of the Chapel be furnished her, and that the Trustees indicate as near as may be when the Chapel will be erected, whether [cinerary] urns can be placed in it, whether it can be known as the Wallace Chapel, and whether the corporation will give her a formal acknowledgement of her gift under its seal.[14]

Mrs. Wallace's request indicates that she intended her donation of the chapel as a memorial to a family member: not only does she desire the chapel be known as the Wallace Chapel, she inquires about the placement of cinerary urns, presumably containing the ashes of the family members memorialized, in the chapel as well.[15]

The trustees did consider seriously Mrs. Wallace's donation, for they inquired about the feasibility of including the chapel in the cathedral program. This request drew a cool response from the cathedral architects, George Louis Heins and Christopher Grant LaFarge. In a letter dated

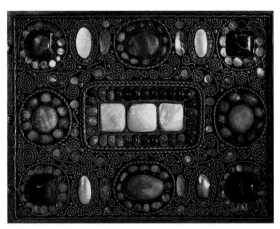

80. Above: Detail of *Tiffany Chapel Altar*, tabernacle door. Brass, gilded lead came, amber, abalone shell, and jade, 11 x 15 1/4 in. (29.8 x 38.7 cm).

78. Previous page, bottom: Detail of *Tiffany Chapel Altar*, St. Luke.

79. Previous page, top: Detail of *Tiffany Chapel Altar*, St. Mark.

September 22, 1896, Heins and LaFarge wrote that after meeting with Tiffany's representative "[i]t [would] not be possible to find a suitable position for the chapel in the part of the Cathedral now under construction." Their letter continues:

We do not wish to make a definitive statement, but it seems to us important to bear constantly in mind, with respect to matters of this sort, that the total effect is of greater consequence than any of the details. It will be recollected that an early study of the interior of the Cathedral was in the Byzantine manner; this the Trustees disapproved and the interior style has been made to correspond with the round arched Gothic style of the exterior. The Tiffany Chapel is in a very pronounced Byzantine style and quite Oriental in its details. It will be seen that it would be out of harmony with the interior of the Cathedral. It would be necessary to take a separate part of the structure, such as the chapel and build it in the Byzantine Style.[16]

Here, Heins and LaFarge voice doubts about incorporating the Tiffany Chapel into the Gothic Revival design of Saint John the Divine, stating that it would detract from the "total effect" of the cathedral. They indicate that the chapel could indeed be incorporated, but that such a consideration would have a financial impact: the added cost of redesigning a part of the cathedral structure in the Byzantine manner to accommodate the chapel. From this letter it is clear that Heins and LaFarge did not want to include the chapel in the cathedral they designed.

Despite the architects' reservations concerning the installation of the chapel, the cathedral accepted Mrs. Wallace's gift. In a letter dated June 1, 1897, Mrs. Wallace confirmed her donation to the cathedral:

Will you permit me to confirm my former gift of the Chapel to the Cathedral of St. John the Divine and to express my willingness to have it used for the crypt as per your conference with Mr. —. The Tiffany glass co hold[s] it subject to your order.[17]

This letter indicates that some compromise was reached between the cathedral and the architects over the siting of the chapel in the cathedral fabric. The agreed upon location was in the crypt beneath the great choir (fig. 81). In the crypt, the "Byzantine," "Oriental" style of the chapel would not interfere with the "Gothic" interior above and the cathedral would have a monumental sacred space for mass, rites and rituals until the completion of the permanent consecrated space above. The installation of the Tiffany Chapel in the Cathedral Church of Saint John the Divine satisfied all involved parties: Mrs. Wallace's familial memorial chapel served one of the most prominent congregations in the Northeast; Saint John the Divine possessed the celebrated Tiffany Chapel unveiled at the 1893 Chicago world's fair; and Heins and LaFarge succeeded in relegating Tiffany's chapel to the basement of their cathedral design.

Preparation of the crypt beneath the choir for the installation of the chapel was completed by the summer of 1898. The Tiffany Glass and Decorating Company delivered the chapel to the cathedral in eighty-one crates from July 25 to August 11, 1898.[18] Within five months of the final crated shipment, the

---

[15] The 1916 guidebook states that the chapel was given in memory of Mrs. Wallace's son; unfortunately, his name is not given. Cathedral League, *Cathedral Church of Saint John the Divine* (New York: St. Bartholomew's Press, 1916), 22.

[16] Heins and LaFarge to George MacCulloch Miller Esq., September 22, 1896, New York.

[17] Mrs. Celia W. Wallace to Bishop Henry Codman Potter, June 1, 1897, New York.

FLOOR PLAN

ST. SAVIOUR

ST. COLUMBA

ST. MARTIN

ST. BONIFACE

ST. AMBROSE

HIGH ALTAR

ST. ANSGAR

NORTH AMBULATORY

ST. JAMES

BIBLICAL GARDEN

GREAT CHOIR

ORGAN SCREEN

ORGAN SCREEN

SOUTH AMBULATORY

CHAPTER HOUSE (as planned)

BAPTISTRY

POETRY WALL

WOMEN

COLUMBARIUM

Pulpit

SOUTH SCREEN

Display Cases

EXHIBIT HALL

NORTH TRANSEPT (unfinished)

CROSSING

MEN

SACRISTIES (not open to public)

Cornerstone laid December 27, 1892.

Structure about two-thirds built.

Length, 601 feet.

Height of Nave Vaulting, 124 feet.

HISTORICAL

ARMED FORCES

ECCLESIASTICAL

RELIGIOUS LIFE

LAWYERS'

NAVE

MEDICAL

EDUCATION

PRESS

CRUSADERS

LABOUR

ARTS

MISSIONARY

SPORTS

ALL SOULS'

NORTH TOWER

NARTHEX

SOUTH TOWER

NORTH PORTAL

CENTRAL PORTAL

SOUTH PORTAL

WEST FRONT

81. Floor plan, The Cathedral Church of Saint John the Divine, begun in 1892. From *The Cathedral Church of Saint John the Divine.* (Charlotte: C. Harrison Conroy Co., Publisher).

Tiffany Chapel was installed completely and consecrated.

The Tiffany Chapel, installed in the crypt beneath the western half of the choir, was entered directly from outside through a door on the east end of the cathedral; the door, no longer extant, was located beneath the present Chapel of St. Savior (fig. 82).[19] Entering the chapel from the east, one would have been confronted immediately with the altar program located on the west wall (fig. 83). What had been an intimate room in Chicago became a decorated wall at Saint John the Divine. With the exception of three windows and the cruciform-shaped electrolier, left in storage because of space restrictions, the chapel was unfolded in fourteen-foot segments against the west crypt wall of the cathedral. The altar, still at the center of the program, was now flanked by two figural windows: to the left the *Angel of the Resurrection* (later redesigned by Tiffany and installed as the *Field of Lilies* in the chapel at Laurelton Hall) and to the right *The Entombment*. The domed baptismal font was located to the left of the altar, appropriately at the feet of the *Angel of the Resurrection*.

As a description appearing in the 1916 guidebook to the cathedral reveals, the monumentality and sumptuous decorative program of the Tiffany Chapel

inspired wonder and awe in the viewer in New York City just as it had in Chicago:

The altar contains 150,000 squares of glass set in mosaic, the top of it and the retable being of Carrara marble, the medallions in front being mother of pearl, and the four smaller disks containing the emblems of the four Evangelists. Sapphires, topazes and pieces of pearl are set in the central shield. The reredos is of iridescent glass mosaic, the font and the lectern are also made of little squares of glass. The twelve pillars back of the altar are of glass mosaic, those nearest it being made up of little crosses. These pillars represent the twelve apostles supporting the arch of Christianity.[20]

The author of this passage is struck by the richness of the west altar wall: the glass mosaic which sheaths the altar, reredos, columns, font, and lectern in shimmering light; the Carrara marble retable; the jewel-encrusted central shield on the altar front. Ironically, this description appeared in print the year the chapel was returned to Louis Comfort Tiffany's care.

At 8 a.m. on April 19, 1911 the last service was held in the Tiffany Chapel.[21] The opening of the permanent consecrated space of the crossing and choir above meant the closing of the chapel in the crypt below. With the chapel no longer in service, unchecked water damage took its toll on the architectural and decorative program.[22] In a letter to the bishop dated May 27, 1916, Tiffany voiced his concern about damage to the chapel he designed and urged that conservation measures be taken:

82. Louis Comfort Tiffany. Tiffany Glass and Decorating Company. *Tiffany Chapel* at The Cathedral Church of Saint John the Divine, ca. 1899. Archival photograph, The Cathedral Church of Saint John the Divine.

[18] Tiffany Glass and Decorating Company to Cathedral Church of Saint John the Divine, eight receipts dated July 25, July 26, July 28, July 30, August 1, August 2, August 11, 1898.

[19] Conversation with Cindi Yoder, Communications, Cathedral Church of Saint John the Divine, June 20, 1996.

[20] Cathedral League, *Cathedral Church of Saint John the Divine* (New York: St. Bartholomew's Press, 1916), 22.

[21] Ibid.

83. Altar program detail, *Tiffany Chapel*, ca. 1899. Archival photograph, The Cathedral Church of Saint John the Divine.

through dampness and neglect, the mosaic work has suffered materially, and as I consider it some of my best work it is but natural that I should feel that some immediate action should be taken for its permanent preservation.

To this end, I am willing, at my own expense, to remove the chancel and its furnishings—restore the same completely—and to hold it until such time as a permanent location has been provided in which it can be placed for services, or until the Cathedral authorities might wish to relinquish it.[23]

The tone of Tiffany's letter indicates that, at the very least, he was annoyed with what he calls the "abandonment" of his chapel. It is reasonable to assume that he may have perceived the neglect of the chapel as a slight, for he makes clear in the beginning of his letter that he understood the chapel was to become one of the permanent chapels in the main part of the cathedral. At the

time of his writing, the chapel had been closed for just over five years and essentially left to ruin.

The cathedral did comply with Tiffany's request to remove the chapel, restore and "hold it" until a permanent location could be found. In a letter to Bishop Greer, Tiffany writes that he "shall be glad to start the removal of the chancel on Wednesday, June 7."[24] In a second letter Edwin Stanton George, Tiffany's press man, writes to the dean of the cathedral reconfirming the chapel removal.[25]

With these letters, the correspondence between Tiffany and the Cathedral Church of Saint John the Divine concerning the Tiffany Chapel ends. The Tiffany Chapel was dismantled and removed from the crypt almost seventeen years to the date of its first crated arrival at the cathedral. In 1935, two years after Tiffany died, the cathedral officially relinquished the chapel to the Tiffany Foundation.[26]

[22] Moisture in the crypt was and still is a constant problem. There are two letters from 1903 and 1905 which make reference to the ill effects of moisture on the organ.

[23] Louis Comfort Tiffany to Bishop David H. Greer, May 26, 1916, New York.

[24] Louis Comfort Tiffany to Bishop David H. Greer, June 2, 1916, New York.

[25] Edwin Stanton George to Dean Grosvenor, June 2, 1916, New York.

[26] Judith Johnson, unpublished chronology, March 8, 1979, Archives of Saint John the Divine, New York.

The Challenge of CONSERVATION

by RUSTIN LEVENSON AND JOHN MASEMAN

The conservation treatment of the Tiffany Chapel posed an enormous challenge. The passage of forty years since the deinstallation at Louis Comfort Tiffany's Laurelton Hall estate, the extensively damaged material, and the unevenness of early documentation left a complicated trail of information. Close examination of existing old photographs and study of the physical evidence of the chapel elements were the primary guides to Tiffany's intent as well as the basis for curatorial and conservation decisions.

Beyond intricacies of interpretation were the substantial physical challenges of treatment and installation. The fragile condition of the chapel elements presented complex technical and structural difficulties within the chapel elements as well as in their attachment to the space created for them in the new wing of The Charles Hosmer Morse Museum of American Art.

These aspects of research, documentation, hands-on treatment, installation, and conservation planning consumed more than two years before the opening of the chapel at the Morse Museum in the spring of 1999. All conservation efforts were finally completed the following summer.

Because the chapel had been installed in several locations since 1893, it was important to determine base lines of reference regarding both Tiffany's vision and the practical issues of reassembly.

A team of conservators, curators, art and architectural historians, and architects decided that the conservation should be based primarily on the Laurelton Hall installation because too much of the chapel material from the earlier versions in the exposition and the Cathedral Church of Saint John the Divine had been lost or damaged and replaced by Tiffany in 1916. For installation in the low-ceilinged crypt at Saint John the Divine the entire original upper sections of the arches from the exposition were eliminated so the crypt could accommodate the material. This abbreviated version of the chapel also eliminated the spectacular electrolier. Furthermore, during the last years at Saint John the Divine, the chapel suffered much damage.

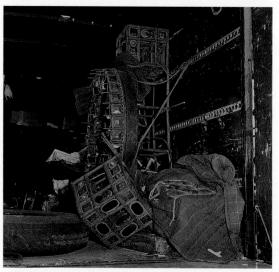

84. Arrival of dismantled *Tiffany Chapel Electrolier* in jumbled condition at the Morse Gallery of Art, Winter Park, 1958. Archival photograph, Morse Museum of American Art.

learly, Louis Comfort Tiffany based his Laurelton Hall reinstallation squarely on the exposition, rather than on the truncated Saint John the Divine chapel. It is evident that in order to reinstall the chapel at Laurelton Hall, he undertook the restoration and replication of many rich sections of the 1893 chapel. Minor differences between the first and last installations are reflected primarily in material that had been lost, sold, or irretrievably damaged in the interim such as the railing, the turtle-back hanging globes, the altar cross, and four altar vessels. Windows were also changed. Changes to the *Field of Lilies* window are described in detail by conservationist Tom Venturella in the chapter "A Major Window Is Restored."

As conservation work progressed, other differences between the world's fair and Laurelton Hall installations were identified by comparing the Joseph Lauber chromolithograph with the Laurelton Hall material at the Morse Museum. These differences were confirmed by examining physical evidence provided by cross sections from chapel material especially at the perimeter of arch six. It was concluded that in the earlier installation, the arches were golden in color and the vaulted ceiling was an earth red. In the later installation the arches may have been cooler silver in tone and the vaulted ceiling may have been a lighter cream color at some time.

All the material at the Morse Museum, having been acquired from Laurelton Hall, was made up of components of the 1893 chapel and the restored and replicated components of the 1916 chapel.

Understanding the history and condition of the various chapel elements in the Laurelton Hall installation was the first step in the conservation process. The chapel was installed in 1916 and until Louis Comfort

Tiffany's death in 1933, was probably well maintained. After 1933 its condition deteriorated as it sustained damage from a leaking roof, vandals, and neglect. It was also during this period that some of the windows and the furnishings were dispersed.

In 1959 Hugh McKean and his wife, Jeannette Genius McKean, purchased the remaining architectural elements of the chapel. They included the columns, the arches, the electrolier, the reredos, the flooring and walls, and the steps and risers. After the purchase, Hugh McKean made arrangements for packing and shipping the pieces from New York to Florida.

Unfortunately, his instructions were not carried out, and the newly acquired material arrived at the Morse jumbled and unprotected in the back of a moving van (fig. 84). There was such extensive damage to some of the chapel elements in the truck that Hugh McKean almost refused shipment. It was certainly the repair of this damage in transit that required the most treatment time by conservators.

The McKeans acquired the remaining major chapel elements in 1963 and from 1973 to 1975. In 1974 D'Eletto Church Interiors of New Jersey restored the altar and lectern and constructed oak platforms for the baptismal font, the altar, and the lectern. Lamb Studios rewired the candlesticks and the altar cross and refurbished the *Madonna and Child* win-

dow. Many of these pieces were exhibited in a Louis Comfort Tiffany exhibit that circulated in the 1970s.

Meanwhile, at the Morse Gallery, which was later to become the Morse Museum of American Art, the electrolier and the reredos were separated from the rest of the material that arrived in the truck and were treated by the Morse. The electrolier was reassembled and repaired. The reredos was reinforced with fiberglass and injected foam and mounted with a wooden framework for display and shipping. Minor additional treatment of the chapel windows was carried out by the Morse as required. The remainder of the lushly decorated architectural setting, the arches, columns, floor, risers, and dark stone walls, was crated and remained in storage for forty more years.

In 1997 the Morse began the chapel conservation and reassembly project. Two years earlier the Museum had moved into a larger facility and was now prepared to add a wing to house the chapel. A temporary conservation laboratory was set up in the Museum's former building. Crates containing the sections of the arches and columns and loose pieces of mosaic and marble were brought out of storage and were arranged in an open space created in the back area of the facility. Old newspapers, straw, and plaster dust littered the area as the fragile, broken pieces were lifted from the crates and placed on ethafoam padding. Once unpacked, the pieces represented a shattered and confusing three-dimensional puzzle.

The structural materials and techniques used by Tiffany to support the artistic surfaces were those that were commonly used in architectural decoration at the turn of the century. The arches were formed by cast plaster reinforced with burlap cloth and metal rods and sealed with shellac. Wooden armatures with joins and carpentry typical of the period formed the structural

support behind the arches. Cutting and dressing of the marble elements reflected traditional techniques.

The elegant arches framing the chapel were decorated with metal leaf, paint, Favrile glass, mother-of-pearl, and pigmented shellac glazes. The composition of the metal leaf was of particular interest. Analysis of the metal leaf carried out at State University of New York Buffalo revealed that the leafing that Tiffany used on the arches was aluminum. Historically, it is important to note the artist's choice of this "modern" material. Aluminum was just beginning to be produced in quantity when the chapel was constructed. At the time of the 1893 world's fair, it was considered a high-quality, innovative, desirable material. Final finishes on the leafing included pigmented shellac and painted surfaces (fig. 85).

As the pieces were treated, the conservators came to understand more about Tiffany's intent. It was evident that he embellished the assembled chapel with glazes to create dramatic chiaroscuro. This can be seen clearly by following the tonality of the entablature which sits between the columns and the arches. The toning in the interior area of the entablature adjoining

85. *Tiffany Chapel* arch detail showing metal leaf finished with pigmented shellac.

the reredos is much darker than in the areas above the outer columns. Similarly, the interior arches have been given a darker toning than the outer arches adding to the air of Byzantine mystery that the chapel in its entirety evokes.

The designs and decorative materials on the arches emphasize Tiffany's attention to detail and his focus on the sanctity of the altar and reredos. The outer arch, arch six, is a simple egg-and-dart pattern in cast plaster, aluminum leafed and toned with pigmented shellac.

Arch five, an aluminum-leafed, convex, cast-plaster arch, was decorated with green glass beads and glass balls. The roundels in arch five are embellished with Celtic designs and Maltese crosses. Complex serpentine patterns decorate the remainder of the arch surface. The keystone in the center of arch five over the altar is a scroll-ended cross decorated with green glass elements. In an elegant intimate detail, one of the glass balls near the keystone cross contains a three-dimensional flower design (fig. 86).

Arch four is a flat, painted-plaster arch inscribed in Latin "+ SANCTVS + SANCTVS + SANCTVS + DOMINVS + DEVS + OMNIPOTENS + QVI ERAT + ET QVI EST + ET QVI VENTVRVS EST +". The letters and the Maltese crosses that intersperse the words are in tex-

86. *Tiffany Chapel* arch detail showing keystone cross and three-dimensional flower design in glass ball.

tured foil behind glass.

Arch three is an aluminum-leafed, cast-plaster, concave arch. Like arch five it features roundels and complex decorations. The cross decorations are more visible in arch three, and the surface is more highly decorated. Favrile glass is used for accenting the decorative elements.

Arch two, another aluminum-leafed, concave arch, has little cast decoration in comparison to arches three and five, but exhibits more lushly decorated roundels. Tiffany uses Favrile glass to depict colorful mosaic crosses in the roundels in arch two.

Arch one, the most interior arch, over the reredos is the most expansively decorated. Cast plaster forms the concave arch. Six spectacular roundels are richly decorated with jewel-like, cast-glass beads and mother-of-pearl. These opulent, colorful decorations form crosses and other religious images. Randomly shaped Favrile glass fragments form mosaic-like decoration around the roundels.

The columns provide another example of Tiffany's masterful craftsmanship. Throughout the chapel, the most minute details are lavished with careful artistic consideration, and the many thousands of mosaic pieces in the columns are no exception. Each tile was created by hand with many layers of glass to achieve specific reflectance and effects. For example, the green color that is visible is produced not by green glass, but by green light reflecting out from the back of the mosaic tesserae through several layers of different colored glass.

Documentation of the columns included mapping the various mosaic designs on the twelve columns of the altar platform. As the detailed drawing and examination took place, conservators could see that Tiffany used his subtly colored tiles to create six

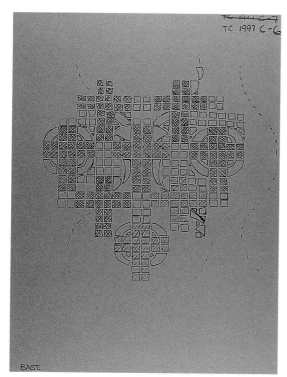

87. Conservation drawing showing cross patterns on *Tiffany Chapel* column.

different column patterns, some incorporating cross patterns (fig. 87). When the individual columns were located within the chapel, it was clear that Tiffany had planned the decoration of the columns in the same way as the arches, with the religious cross motifs increasingly appearing in the mosaic patterns as the columns get closer to the most sacred area at the back

and center of the chapel. There are no crosses visible in the whimsical organic decoration of the four columns at the entry to baptismal area (fig. 88), while crosses dominate the two columns at the rear of the altar area (fig. 89).

Similarly the decoration of the capitals and the step risers exhibit designs of increasing sacredness as the reredos and altar are approached. The simple geometric design of the first risers (fig. 90) evolves through Latin religious inscriptions to the spiritual images on the far risers (fig. 91).

The altar furnishings are also a testimony to Tiffany's creative ability. The altar itself is white marble decorated with mosaic. The altar emblems of the four evangelists are composed of mother-of-pearl and cast-glass elements. On the altar was a metal-wire-and-glass cross created by Tiffany for the Laurelton Hall installation. Also on the altar were four of six original candle-

89. Above: *Tiffany Chapel* column detail showing use of colored mosaic to create cross design.

88. Left: *Tiffany Chapel* column detail showing random mosaic pattern.

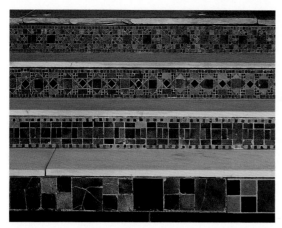

90. *Tiffany Chapel* step risers detail showing geometric tile designs.

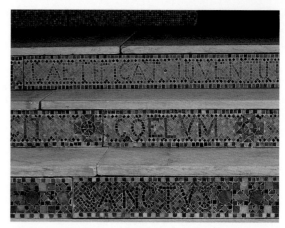

91. *Tiffany Chapel* detail of Latin religious inscriptions in tile on final step risers leading to altar.

sticks from the world's fair installation fabricated of a metal tube painted with gold. The tabernacle door on the altar is formed of metal grillwork with inset stones. The reredos is composed of iridescent glass mosaic. The baptismal font, the candlesticks at the lectern, and the lectern itself are made of marble and glass tesserae.

Working closely with the original chapel material, conservators documented many examples of Tiffany's skillful manipulation of light, color, and design to enhance the mystery and spiritual sense of the chapel.

The first step in the conservation process was to begin the extensive documentation that would continue through the project. Pieces were drawn, measured, assessed, and photographed. The photographs of the arch sections were cropped and reassembled to determine whether elements were missing. Fortunately, although many of the architectural pieces were badly damaged, no major portion was missing. In fitting the sections of the arches together, an extra plaster piece was discovered. It had traveled to the Morse with the chapel in 1959. This darkened decorative piece appears to be a casting mold made to create replacement pieces that were used for Tiffany's Laurelton Hall restora-

tion. Initial study and measurements of the chapel components were also important for integrating the design and architectural layout of the chapel.

Beyond the large-puzzle aspects of the chapel elements were the pieces that were dubbed the "truck sweepings." Hugh McKean had instructed that every fragment on the floor of the truck be saved. The conservators' "packing-crate sweepings" were added to the "truck sweepings" and included hundreds of mosaic pieces, stones, a cigar box, old newspapers, and bits of metal and plaster (fig. 92). Part of the conservation process included patient sorting of these elements and

92. Conservator John Maseman sorting chapel shards.

93. Conservator John Maseman replacing glass "jewel" in partially reconstructed capital of chapel column.

placing as many of them as possible back into the arches, risers, and columns (fig. 93).

The varied chapel components had unique conservation requirements. A great deal of detailed work was required to bring the chapel elements to the point where they could be aesthetically and structurally reassembled.

Actual treatment of the chapel began with careful cleaning of each piece, vacuuming, dusting with soft brushes, then cleaning with a mild non-ionic detergent solution and distilled water using small cotton swabs (fig. 94). Relieving the chapel elements of the dust and dirt of the ages improved their appearance considerably. After cleaning, the pieces of columns and arches came to life, revealing subtle color and detail that had been lost for years.

Consolidation of the chapel elements was the next step. The arches were initially consolidated with Rhoplex AC234 at the damaged areas. Small fragments were reattached with B-72 acrylic copolymer. Stainless steel rods were used as dowels to join larger fragments and the backs of large joins were reinforced with Pemaco brand Ortho Plaster. The localized missing areas of the arches were more problematic. Casts were made with silicone rubber and Ortho Plaster to fill missing areas. These were attached in place with a B-72 copolymer, reinforced with connecting dowels

and/or on the reverse with materials such as wood, fabric, or plaster. Losses were neutrally toned with acrylic paint.

Broken areas of the columns were joined with stainless steel dowels and B-72 adhesive. Laboratory plaster was used for reinforcement on the reverse. Dental wax molds were used to cast missing pieces which were placed into the areas of loss and reinforced with burlap strips or stainless steel rods. The columns were further stabilized with top and bottom steel plates connected with a threaded rod. These served the dual purpose of securing the columns and of helping support the weight of the entablature. Retouching of the columns was limited to neutral toning of the areas of damage except in large areas of loss where the design was re-created.

The floors and walls were surface cleaned with a non-ionic detergent in water. Missing sections of marble were replaced with modern marble. Missing areas of the black stone wall surface were infilled with solid-surface sheet material.

The step risers were consolidated with Rhoplex AC234. Missing riser pieces were formed of Ortho Plaster cast in metal-lined wooden molds. Using historic photographs, the mosaic pattern was re-created and repainted with acrylic media paints.

The reredos was surface cleaned, and the old mount was partially removed in order to prepare for reintegration of the upper perimeter with arch one.

The windows, the altar, the chapel door, the baptismal font, and other chapel fixtures were surface cleaned and excess filling removed. The restored *Field of Lilies* window was mounted in a metal frame. Once all the elements were treated and stabilized, the next step was the reassembly of the chapel in the new wing of the Museum.

94. Conservator cleaning tesserae on chapel lectern.

Because of the limitations in the final access to the chapel, the larger elements had to be moved in and installed while a wall was still open. The electrolier, altar, and baptismal font were brought into the area and protected with plywood crates.

Conservator John Maseman created laminated plywood arches designed to match exactly the shape of Tiffany's six arches. They were suspended from the ceiling by adjustable rods (fig. 95). Each repaired section of plaster arch was carefully attached in place beginning with the keystone in arch five. Thin ethafoam was cut in the profile of each arch and used as a spacer between the separate arch pieces to prevent damage. Final adjustments and leveling of the support arches were done with the threaded suspension rods.

The altar, the baptismal font, the columns, and the floor were supported by a specially constructed wooden platform. The floor fragments were set in place, but were not attached to the wooden platform. Access to this area will be strictly controlled to prevent further damage to the marble flooring. Wall pieces were attached to a supporting wooden framework with screws through historic holes.

The electrolier was hung in place with a chain, and the windows were mounted in light boxes with individual air-conditioning supply-and-return vents.

The reassembly of the chapel required involvement with architects and contractors to help integrate the chapel safely into a newly constructed space. Many aspects of the construction impacted the long-term stability of the chapel.

Educational aspects of the conservation of the chapel included not only giving tours of the laboratory to Museum staff and docents, but also guiding working relationships with contractors and subcontractors to engender enthusiasm and cooperation with conservation goals.

Treatment documents of the chapel conservation will be the basis for study, conservation, and care of the chapel for years to come. The conservators' reports will provide detailed information to scholars studying Tiffany's materials and techniques. Information in the reports also will be valuable to those doing future conservation. Finally, documentation includes guidance to Museum staff for chapel maintenance and deinstallation should that ever be required.

95. Museum staff adjusting chapel arch section to fit its plywood mount.

A Major Window Is PRESERVED

by TOM VENTURELLA

The Angel of the Resurrection *window exhibited in the Tiffany Chapel at the World's Columbian Exposition in Chicago depicted a loggia consisting of a low retaining wall on which four square columns with acanthus-style capitals stood upholding a jeweled entablature. In the center of the window was the figure of an angel in the foreground and lilies in the distance. It was exhibited in the chapel baptistery behind the baptismal font.*

After the exposition the chapel was removed to Tiffany's Fourth Avenue studios in New York. It was purchased by Mrs. Celia Whipple Wallace of Chicago and donated to the Cathedral Church of Saint John the Divine in New York City. As explained in other chapters, it was installed in the crypt as the nave was not yet built. When Tiffany repossessed the chapel and furnishings in 1916 he had them installed in an outbuilding on his property at Laurelton Hall. It was at this time that he redesigned the Angel of the Resurrection *window for its new location, renaming it* Field of Lilies *(fig. 96). The leaded center panel depicting the angel and the two columns flanking it were removed. Two new round columns were designed to match the mosaic-encrusted ones which supported the six jeweled arches in the chapel, and the angel was replaced with a full field of copper-foiled lilies. The extreme left and right original square columns and lilies immediately adjacent to them, all remained. At this time there are no records as to the fate of either the angel or the two square columns that flanked her. It was not uncommon for Tiffany to make changes to windows, especially those of his own design and certainly those with which he chose to live. This new* Field of Lilies *was once again placed behind the baptismal font.*

The Field of Lilies *was acquired by the Morse in 1958 and moved to Winter Park. By 1998 sections of the window were buckling due to an inherent design flaw that in turn caused the support system to fail. This condition was exacerbated by previous repairs that adversely affected the window aesthetically and structurally.*

This large window is approximately eleven and one-half feet high by nine feet wide and is horizontally separated into two panels at the center. Its outstanding features include the use of drapery glass in the floral areas, a band of cabochon jewels across the top of the entablature (the area above the columns), and the use of multiple layers of glass (plates) to create nuances of color and depth. A non-fired paint layer (cold paint) was generously applied to many areas of the window including large plates across the back, as well as surfaces of selected pieces of glass within the plating system. Similar to plating, this technique is used to control the amount of light coming through the window. Modulating color and creating special effects with acid-etched glass was a trademark of Tiffany's work in leaded glass. Behind the lilies in the top panel, a piece of French-blue-on-clear glass has areas of blue removed with hydrofluoric acid to expose the clear base glass (fig. 97). These clear areas become highlights of the flowers while the

97. *Field of Lilies* window disassembled for conservation, detail showing second layer French-blue-on-clear-glass plate.

remaining color deepens the blue background surrounding them. In the area just above, lavender on clear glass is acid etched to create the colorings of sunrise or sunset.

Both top and bottom panels were set in a support system of two large steel vertical bars traversing the center columns through which ran nine horizontal round support bars. Copper wire, soldered to the leads, was tied to these horizontal bars, which held the panels vertically in their frames. Many of these copper tie wires had torn loose from the leads and were uselessly encircling the round support bars allowing the window to buckle under its own weight. This was particularly evident in the bottom panel which was inherently weak due to thirteen repetitive horizontal lines of the low retaining wall on which the four columns stand. As these horizontal lead lines flexed, an accordionated folding condition was set in motion. The resulting buckling was the major structural concern of this window.

The top panel had many pieces of broken glass which had been summarily addressed. These repairs interfered with the visual effect originally intended by Tiffany. For example, broken glass representing sky above the lilies between the two center columns was repaired with either glue or sili-

96. Louis Comfort Tiffany. Tiffany Glass and Decorating Company. *Tiffany Chapel* baptistery showing *Field of Lilies* window at Laurelton Hall chapel installation, 1930s.

cone and lead flanges (strips of lead laid across the breaks and soldered in place). In the center of the window, a large vertical lead flange was soldered to the leads of the back plate above the lilies while a number of flange repairs were made to the glass plate just above it. This created an overall spider-web effect (fig. 98) in an area which was, as a focal point, designed to be tranquil and calm. On the front, the large center sky plates had been removed for repair. When replaced, they were set in front of the horizontal reinforcing bars rather than behind as originally designed. This left the uppermost plate tilting awkwardly forward which created an unsightly thick, dark line due to the clumsy looking repair leads. In the entablature, areas of original lead had been replaced with leads of different profiles creating an interrupted visual linear flow. Dirt had accumulated between plates throughout the window and darkened some areas, prohibiting any transmission of light. As the tie wires gave way and the panels began to buckle, some leads were torn, and numerous solder joints cracked.

The first matter of concern was the removal of both panels from their frames. While they had the steel reinforcing system on the front, the perimeter framing members of the panels were made of wood. Within these wood-and-steel-combination frames, the panels were extremely flexible, which made moving them precarious. The panels were laid on two-inch, foam-covered boards with the barring system face up. Tie wires still holding were cut, bars were removed, and the remaining framing system was lifted off the glass allowing the panels to settle onto the foam beds. Broken plates between the center columns in the top panel were carefully numbered and removed. There were as

many as three, and sometimes more, layers of glass in these areas making up the sky above the lilies (fig. 99). Glass was cleaned as plates were removed for repair. Selected interior surfaces of some plates within the entablature had been cold painted. These fragile surfaces were cleaned by dusting lightly with a soft bristle brush. Where necessary, previous repair leads and flanges were removed and broken glass edges glued with silicone. Six non-original small, flat bars that had been soldered to the entablature were removed as they were unsightly and provided no additional support. In this area leads of incorrect profile from previous repairs were skimmed back. New flanges were soldered to the hearts and the front surface of the lead floated with solder to re-create the look of the surrounding original lead

98. Louis Comfort Tiffany. Tiffany Glass and Decorating Company. *Field of Lilies* window, ca. 1892/1916, showing flange repairs before conservation. Leaded Favrile glass, 134 x 110 in. (340.4 x 279.4 cm). Morse Museum of American Art (U-071).

(fig. 100). Numerous broken solder joints through-out the top panel were scraped clean and resol-dered. New lead channels surrounding the repaired plates allowed the horizontal round bars to be set between the plates as originally designed. New tie wires replaced the originals, and additional wires were placed along the two center columns. The leads of the round columns in both top and bottom panels were tied to the large, flat vertical steel bars.

The bottom panel contained large areas of lilies, the two end panels leaded and the center panel copper-foiled. All three areas were very stable and solid. As the column-supporting low retaining wall was buckling, wires tied to the bars were tear-ing free from the leads. Glass between the center

99. Disassembled *Field of Lilies* window, sky detail, showing three layers of paneling.

column bases was removed to allow for the straightening of leads. Flattening the leads was achieved through gentle, even pressure applied with weights (fig. 101). Lead hearts and flanges were rebuilt and broken glass was silicone-edge glued, then reset into the newly straightened leads. In order to compensate for the inherent design weak-ness of this section, two additional flat steel rein-forcing bars were added. These new bars were bent to conform to the inner profiles of the square columns, and continued down the panel crossing the thirteen horizontal lines of the wall. Holes were then drilled to allow the passing through of the horizontal round bars that in turn anchor into the frame. The new flat bars were soldered to the front of the panel. These, in addition to the new tie wires (including those now on the center columns), hold the panel in a vertical position in the frame. The wood-and-steel-combination frames did not provide adequate support for the two panels that make up this window. Frames were designed using original steel members to which steel angles were added, replacing the wooden members, and welded to the original vertical flat steel bars. Thus a non-flexing framing system was created.

Large glass plates covered the entire back of the window. The purpose was to tone the light being transmitted, and many of these plates had the additional application of cold paint. Three dark gray plates covered the entablature, the center plate broken in many pieces. It had been glued during a previous repair and some of the glue joints had failed. Where this had happened, the plate was repaired with copper-foil lines thin enough not to be visible from the front. The low retaining wall under the columns was covered with two layers of large, dark-gray plates. Some surfaces contained cold paint while others did not. Some faced in while others faced out. The two broken plates in this group were repaired in the same copper-foil manner as the plates in the entablature. Large, bulky leads holding these plates (applied in a previous repair) were replaced with lead of the correct smaller profiles, consistent with original leads on the back of the window. Before the cleaned and repaired glass plates were replaced,

many broken joints were resoldered, and exposed back surfaces of the window were cleaned.

The newly modified steel frames were set over the restored panels as they lay face up on the foam boards. The round horizontal bars were reset and the framed panels lifted to the vertical position. All wires were tied and trimmed while new solder joints were brushed to darken them. With access to both sides of the panels, final cosmetic cleaning was possible.

The newly restored *Field of Lilies* window was installed in the reassembled Tiffany Chapel at the Morse Museum in November 1998 looking much as it did when installed at Laurelton Hall in 1916.

101. Conservator Susan Greenbaum flattening leads through pressure applied with weights on bottom panel of *Field of Lilies* window.

100. Conservator Thomas Venturella soldering around lead to re-create look of surrounding original lead in entabulature area of *Field of Lilies* window.

About the CONTRIBUTORS

ALICE COONEY FRELINGHUYSEN is the Anthony W. and Lulu Wang curator, Department of American Decorative Arts at The Metropolitan Museum of Art in New York City. She has a B.A. degree from the Department of Art and Archaeology, Princeton University and a M.A. degree from the Winterthur Program in Early American Culture. Having published and lectured widely on the work of Louis Comfort Tiffany, she has curated numerous Tiffany exhibitions and authored or co-authored *Splendid Legacy: The Havemeyer Collection; American Porcelain, 1770-1920;* and *In Pursuit of Beauty: Americans and the Aesthetic Movement.*

WENDY KAPLAN is department head and curator, Decorative Arts, Los Angeles County Museum of Art in California. She has B.A. and M.A. degrees in American civilization from the University of Pennsylvania and a M.A. degree from the Winterthur Program in Early American Culture. Invited to speak internationally on various aspects of the decorative arts, she authored *Leading "The Simple Life": The Arts and Crafts Movement in Britain, 1880-1910;* co-authored *The Arts and Crafts Movement;* and was editor and principal author of *"The Art that is Life": The Arts and Crafts Movement in America, 1875-1920.*

JOEL M. HOFFMAN is vice-director, Education and Program Development, Brooklyn Museum of Art in New York City. He holds a Ph.D. in art history from Yale University, and his publications include an article on the representation of Florida in United States world's fairs in *The Journal of Decorative and Propaganda Arts* that focuses on the holdings of The Wolfsonian-Florida International University.

RUSTIN LEVENSON is director of Rustin Levenson Art Conservation Associates, New York City and Miami. She has a B.A. degree in art history from Wellesley College and received conservation training at Harvard University's Fogg Art Museum. Having published extensively in conservation and art history journals, she also co-authored *Seeing through Paintings.*

JOHN MASEMAN is director and chief conservator, South Florida Conservation Center. He holds B.A. degrees in ancient history and natural sciences from the University of South Florida and a B.Sc. degree in objects conservation from the University of London, Institute of Archaeology, United Kingdom. He was project training conservator for the State of Florida's SAVE OUTDOOR SCULPTURE survey.

PATRICIA PONGRACZ SPICKA is curator, The Gallery at the American Bible Society in New York. She holds a B.A. degree in English literature from College of the Holy Cross and a M.A. in the history of art and architecture from Brown University. A Ph.D. candidate in the history of art and architecture at Brown, she has contributed articles on art and architecture for catalogues and magazines.

THOMAS VENTURELLA is the owner and operator of Venturella Studio in New York City where he has been working solely with stained and leaded glass since 1969. He holds a B.F.A. degree in painting from the School of The Art Institute of Chicago and is a member of the American Institute for Conservation and the International Institute for Conservation. Having done extensive conservation and restoration work on windows by Tiffany Studios, he has lectured and written widely about stained glass.